Science Fiction
in Classic Rock

Critical Explorations in Science Fiction and Fantasy
(a series edited by Donald E. Palumbo and C.W. Sullivan III)

Science Fiction in Classic Rock

Musical Explorations of Space, Technology and the Imagination, 1967–1982

ROBERT MCPARLAND

CRITICAL EXPLORATIONS
IN SCIENCE FICTION AND FANTASY, 59
Series Editors Donald E. Palumbo *and* C.W. Sullivan III

McFarland & Company, Inc., Publishers
Jefferson, North Carolina

LIBRARY OF CONGRESS CATALOGUING-IN-PUBLICATION DATA

Names: McParland, Robert, author.
Title: Science fiction in classic rock : musical explorations of space, technology and the imagination, 1967–1982 / Robert McParland.
Description: Jefferson, North Carolina : McFarland & Company, 2017. | Series: Critical explorations in science fiction and fantasy ; 59 | Includes bibliographical references and index.
Identifiers: LCCN 2017041520 | ISBN 9781476664705 (softcover : acid free paper) ∞
Subjects: LCSH: Rock music—History and criticism. | Science fiction in music.
Classification: LCC ML3534 .M472 2017 | DDC 781.66—dc23
LC record available at https://lccn.loc.gov/2017041520

BRITISH LIBRARY CATALOGUING DATA ARE AVAILABLE

ISBN (print) 978-1-4766-6470-5
ISBN (ebook) 978-1-4766-3030-4

Front cover image © 2017 iStock

Printed in the United States of America

McFarland & Company, Inc., Publishers
Box 611, Jefferson, North Carolina 28640
www.mcfarlandpub.com

Table of Contents

Preface

Science fiction and rock music have been involved in a dynamic relationship since the late 1960s. Rock's relationship with myth goes back even further, for myth has been a source of wonder and story in the human imagination since ancient times. The presence of science fiction imagery in psychedelic rock, progressive rock, and heavy metal has been part of the rock music experience of many listeners. Yet, few studies have explored the relationship between these popular arts, or have probed the mythical imagination of rock music. This book is a descriptive survey: a sketch of classic rock's engagement with myth and with science fiction. It begins with the premise that as we undergo significant technological change in our time we carry with us the ancient, the primeval, and indeed the mythical strands of human experience in a new social, technological, and cultural context.

The discussion that follows is presented in non-technical language, so that this book can be easily digested by readers who are not sociologists, musicologists, or cultural critics. This is a selective discussion, which is by no means an exhaustive inquiry into this subject. Nor is it intended as an analytical study of the compositions of the artists referred to here. My goal is simply to invite you to listen to and reflect upon the music, concepts, and imagery of a few commercially successful bands who have made use of myth and science fiction. These are bands whose most lasting work was created in the late 1960s, the 1970s, and the early to mid–1980s. The work of these artists has been amply documented and they have produced a good deal of critical and biographical information. With the exception of Hawkwind, or other early participants in the "space rock" genre, I omit cult bands and do not develop this discussion in relation to heavy metal or alternative music of the late 1980s into the 1990s and in this century.

Preface

Myth pervades popular culture: from rock music to television and from comics to film. A study of popular culture and its artifacts can provide us with insight into the social concerns and cultural thought and attitudes of a given time. Myth and science fiction motifs will likely continue to appear in the work of rock music artists and bands. This study investigates their assertion of imagination and individuality and the relationship of their music with mythology and with science fiction. It pursues an inquiry into how rock songwriters and performers utilize the mythical themes of heroism and journey and the monstrous or fantastic and how they direct their attention to social issues, technological wonders, and projections of the future.

Following an introduction, the first chapter provides a brief overview of some of the bands and artists who have created works that have engaged with myth or science fiction. The second chapter is a bit more theoretical and looks at creativity, the importance of myth, and at science fiction. Subsequent chapters deal with rock music artists who have utilized science fiction or myth in their work: the Jefferson Starship, ELO, Pink Floyd, David Bowie, Blue Öyster Cult, Rush, and the Alan Parsons Project.

I would like to invite you to listen to the recordings considered here and to read the science fiction texts that are mentioned. A bibliography will direct you to rewarding studies of these artists. While I was writing this book we lost David Bowie, Keith Emerson, and Paul Kantner. This book is written in thanks for their remarkable creativity and it is dedicated to science fiction readers and to avid rock music listeners, who can obviously say much more about how these fascinating artists, books, and recordings have touched their lives than I ever could.

Wishing you good listening.

Introduction

When the lights come up on a rock concert stage it is as if the sky has opened in a burst of solar energy. The sound of guitars rises over the long chords from keyboards, the pulse of a bass run, and the first sharp hits of the drums. Then a concert is born, like a moment of creation in cosmic thunder, and a voice breaks through to tell us a strange, mythical story. Rock and science fiction appear this way: as spectacle and sound, technologically driven music, imagery, and lyrics that refer to wondrous worlds.

So, buckle up. Put your headphones on. The countdown has begun. We are going to take off into imaginative journeys and speculative fiction with some of the finest rock acts in existence. Some of the most profound scientific questions about the nature of the universe appear in science fiction stories. Rock musicians and their fans are among the thousands of people who are fascinated with these stories and are asking these questions. Science fiction and mythological speculations appear in the work of Rush, Pink Floyd, the Electric Light Orchestra (ELO), Yes, David Bowie, the Moody Blues, Blue Öyster Cult, T. Rex, Hawkwind, Iron Maiden, Emerson, Lake, and Palmer, the Alan Parsons Project, Genesis, Muse, Motörhead, Brian Eno, Jefferson Starship, and many other bands. Rock music is part of the voice of our time and the work of these bands recognizes that our very fate as a species is bound up with science and imagination. Science fiction in rock is a fertile, creative subgenre that reminds us that the staggering advances of science and technology are now deeply connected with the human endeavor. These rock acts have absorbed science fiction in print or on film and have brought the imagery of science fiction to their songs, performances, and album imagery. We will look at how these rock music artists draw upon science fiction literature, film, and mythology to create their popular music.

Introduction

The science fiction genre has intersected with rock in one hit wonders like Zager and Evans' "In the Year 2525," popular hit singles like Elton John's "Rocket Man," and in dazzling instrumentals like Edgar Winter's "Frankenstein." In the age of the LP recording, science fiction imagery graced album covers, projecting the futuristic worlds of progressive bands like Rush and Yes, creating the androgynous Ziggy Stardust character of David Bowie, and visually expressing the imaginative vision of Boston and heavy metal bands like Iron Maiden. Science fiction may, likewise, be said to be in the sound of some of these artists. Conceptually, it registers in the expansion of keyboard sounds from synthesizers to the experimental lines of soaring guitars and throughout studio effects by which musicians and producers sculpt albums.

Rock artists have been drawn toward science fiction because it is one of the most progressive of fiction genres. Science fiction is rich in imagination. It supports the urge to envision possibilities. Stories of science fiction promote reflection and social critique. In this sense, science fiction is a voice of counterculture that is willing to break with convention and explore uniqueness, novelty, and the reaches of human consciousness. In this respect, it is parallel with the quest of some our world's most creative rock visionaries. These musicians are exploring the reaches of sound, image, recording technology, and the human story.

Rock musicians draw upon myths, which are the oldest form of human imagination. Science fiction is involved with myths and mythic patterns, while responding to modernity, or imaginative visions of the future. Science fiction seeks alternative realities and societal possibilities. There are rock performers who recognize how myth is used to construct future models of reality. With their propensity for imaginative vision, these rock composers borrow from myth. What are explored here are the science fiction themes and mythological themes that appear in the songs of these artists. In some cases, these come from their reading, or from their viewing science fiction movies, or from television shows that they have seen. However, it is wrong to say that these songs are simply derivative of such sources. Rather, these works of creative imagination arise from the unique talents of these artists, at times from an archetypal and mythological level of consciousness. They emerge from their music, their feelings and emotions, their personal experiences, and perhaps from hallucinatory drug use, in some cases. Open to cultural resources, including books and film, the rock musician makes culture as he or she seeks alternative worlds.

Mythology offers a rich repository of stories and images. Sir James Frazer, in *The Golden Bough* (1890), showed us that the stories and images which arise in these ancient myths have similarities across cultures. Myths and their heroes are something more than ways to dramatize natural phenomena that cannot be explained otherwise. They are expressions of cultural understanding, aspirations, and fundamental patterns of life. The psychologist Carl Jung believed that deep within the collective unconscious of the human race there are common images. These figures he referred to as archetypes.[1] The German ethnologist Adolf Bastian (1826–1905) asserted that the human imagination seems to be constituted in such a way that it works with certain shapes, images, themes, and elemental ideas. These archetypes continue to appear in our songs, in our imagery, and in our performance rituals.

The quest of a hero, exotic lands, alien beings, and strange places and characters make up motifs that appear in rock album concepts and lyrics. These worlds arise from mythological designs, whether the landscape is pastoral and agrarian, or highly technological. Joseph Campbell, in his fascinating study *The Hero with a Thousand Faces* (1949), identified the monomyth: a universal story pattern. In this story, the hero is called to adventure, experiences an initiation and rising fortunes, then faces what Aristotle called *peripeteia*, or a reversal of fortunes. Heroes face monsters, twisting plots, fierce conflicts, and they make thrilling escapes. When all seems lost, against impossible odds, the hero emerges. From imminent loss, constriction, or imprisonment he or she breaks free, rises to the challenge, and saves the day. The hero, Campbell pointed out, returns with a boon, or gift, to his society.

These figures that live in the roots of human consciousness appear in rock songs and performances. When a rock performer develops a persona he is dealing in archetypes and appealing to this kind of consciousness. In writing lyrics that dwell in fantasy, the rock songwriter is exploring these archetypal depths. The heroic fantasy figure, like the creative artist, is an adventurer, an explorer. At times, he or she is alone, possibly orphaned by society, or socially alienated. This character, however, has unique strengths of emotion, craftiness, or imagination. In this sense, the rock performer may project himself or herself into a heroic fantasy character, as Bruce Dickinson of Iron Maiden has done when singing of great cosmic duels, or as David Bowie has done with his hermaphroditic Ziggy Stardust. The rock performer creates alternative worlds and stages a fictional world in music and performance. The world that is created may seem quite tangible and real. In this respect, the rock music creator is much like the imaginative science fiction writer.

When science fiction themes and motifs have been incorporated into rock music these themes appear most obviously in the lyrics. Yet, they are also evident in the artwork that accompanies albums, or in concert appearances and performance styles. Musical composition, the aural space and the making of a record, as well as electronic effects, lines of melody, tempo, rhythm and key signature change in a band's music are all aspects of their musical art. In the art of the song, themes and motifs have to be considered musically, as well as lyrically. So too does each band's public image. So, make sure to consider these factors as you get hold of the albums, download the MP3s, and start your own exploration of the myths, sounds, and images of science fiction rock.

The variety of these bands is astonishing. Their sounds range from progressive rock to heavy metal and from alternative rock to space rock. What you will discover as you listen to them is a colorful palette of striking imagery and mind-stretching sonic textures. Since the late 1960s, science fiction themed songs have ranged from Pink Floyd's "Interstellar Overdrive" and "Set the Controls for the Heart of the Sun" (1968) to the identity and gender morphing of David Bowie's "Space Oddity" (1969) and from Alan Parsons' references to Isaac Asimov's *I, Robot* to Iron Maiden's use of Orson Scott Card's *Seventh Son* on their album *Seventh Son of a Seventh Son*. Science fiction rock has crossed over from epic length progressive rock forays from Rush, Yes, and Genesis to the heavy metal and alternative rock of the 1990s and 2000s. The Flaming Lips, Radiohead, the Verve, Flying Saucer Attack, Flowers of Hell, Comets of Fire, Angels and Airwaves, and many others have explored myth and sonic textures. The vitality of these bands shows that speculative fiction has been a potent contributor to rock music.

Connecting Rock and Science Fiction

Some bands have taken brief detours into themes of science fiction. Styx, which takes its name after the river of the Underworld, moved from Top 20 singles like "Come Sail Away" (1977) to "Mr. Roboto" (1982). Boston made use of the image of spaceship flying away from earth. Blondie sang "Rapture," the Killers sang "Spaceman," and Soundgarden recorded Chris Cornell's "Black Hole Sun" (1994). Science fiction references have crossed genres too. The Beastie Boys rapped "Intergalactic," singing about a pinch on the neck from *Star Trek*'s Spock. When a prominent funk band performed in 1976, the stage was aglow with a spaceship. This oversized prop represented the mothership, a U.F.O., and it had been created for the Parliament Funkadelic O-Funk Earth tour. Group members joined George Clinton in space outfits.[2] These are spectacles that draw upon science fiction imagery. For other bands, involvement with science fiction themes or mythological concepts has been more of a long-term commitment. Hawkwind played space rock for many years. They introduced their two-disc album, *Space Ritual* (1973), with a laser light show in their concerts. The science fiction escapades of Klaatu are legendary. (Someone started a rumor that Klaatu were The Beatles; the band immediately denied this. None of The Beatles were ever involved with this Canadian band and their space rock imagery.) Gong, an eclectic Franco-British rock band formed in 1967 by Australian Daevid Allen, a member of the band Soft Machine, has had a constantly changing entourage. The band Soft Machine took its name from a William Burroughs science fiction novel, *The Soft Machine*.

Science fiction imagery was alive when David Bowie transformed into Ziggy Stardust, exploring the boundaries of gender and identity. When Rush narrated a story of Cygnus X-1, they were bringing us to imaginative worlds, much like science fiction writers and filmmakers have done. These artists recognized that rock music, as a commercial art form, is very much about creating records that will sell, songs that will get downloaded, concert programs that will sell tickets. However, they also asserted that rock music is about play and rebellion and freedom. Rock is about energy, attitude, sound, and imagery. It breaks through the mundane and transforms the ordinary world, reminding us of magic, of instinct, and of mystery. Rock music's science fiction narrative, like science fiction itself, is about wonder, curiosity, and imaginative inquiry. It is a form of art that taps into the deep resources of mythology, music, theatre, and visual art.

When rock meets with mythology or with science fiction it offers musical expression that reminds us that humanity is fundamentally curious about origins and the mysteries and wonders of the universe. Science and the wide imaginative range of science fiction explore our sense of wonder; they express a curiosity that is a natural impulse within us. The astronomer Johannes Kepler once observed: "We do not ask for what useful purpose the birds do sing, for song is their pleasure since they were created for singing. Similarly, we ought not to ask why the human mind troubles to fathom the secrets of the heavens."[3] Musical imagination is at the center of rock music. It is stimulated by new sounds and creative performances, by stories and imagery. It is given shape in song lyrics and the imagery that artists bring to stage performances and videos. Mythology and the speculation present in science fiction thus have much to contribute to it.

The rock musician in the brave new world of digital technology has turned toward the speculations of science fiction to expand the range of his or her own expressive encounter with modern life. Rush's *Clockwork Angels*, Pink Floyd's *The Dark Side of the Moon*, the Alan Parsons Project's *I Robot*, or Brian Eno's *Another Green World* and *Before and After Science* are examples of rock creations that have stretched the boundaries of sound and music technology. Science fiction has provided them and acts like David Bowie with intriguing performance imagery that can imaginatively light up a stage, a stage persona, or an album concept. Science fiction imagination had been a colorful resource for rock music lyrics and album concepts for Blue Öyster Cult, Rush, the Jefferson Starship, Yes, Boston, and many other rock groups.

The Emergence of Science Fiction

The emergence of science fiction in the twentieth century predates the birth of rock music by several decades. In the first decades of the twentieth century, the pulp magazines of Hugo Gernsback, a scientist-entrepreneur, fostered modern science fiction in America. In the pages of *Amazing Stories*, "scientification" or "scientific fiction" reached a wide public in a seminal publication that was illustrated with imaginative covers by the artist Frank R. Paul. Today's Hugo Awards, science fiction's highest honor, are named after Gernsback. Science fiction imagery owes much to Frank R. Paul, an Austrian architect who tuned his imagination toward future worlds and created more than 150 spectacular magazine covers. The creators of LP album covers and the creators of films drew upon these images. The world of fantasy fiction, meanwhile, appeared in *Weird Tales*. While science fiction embraced the hard science of Gernsback, whose reflections helped to define the field, ancient myths and legends mixed with modern imagination in the realm of fantasy fiction as well. In the *Norton Book of Science Fiction*, Ursula K. Le Guin distinguishes science fiction from fantasy. Then she writes: "Science fiction behaves like fantasy ... in making things up which we know don't exist." Yet, how do we know for sure that they don't?[4]

In the 1930s, the renowned *Amazing Stories* was edited by John W. Campbell. This preceded the birth of all of today's rock music performers. However, some of them have read stories from the "golden age of science fiction" that included the fiction of Isaac Asimov, Robert Heinlein, Lester Del Rey, L. Sprague De Camp, Theodore Sturgeon, A.E. van Vogt and others. In the World War II era, science fiction appeared in the pulp magazines, which had been so popular in the 1930s and stories came to new audiences by radio, newspaper comic strips, feature films, and in motion picture serials. Rock performers who were born in the 1940s and 1950s absorbed juvenile serials and comic books and radio and they experienced science fiction as the field was advanced further by the advent of television, beginning in the 1940s and 1950s. Those born later, from the 1960s through the 1980s, have seen science fiction stories enter the literary mainstream and extend across the world in film. With the 1970s, science fiction, once a genre eschewed by many literary critics, gained further respect. It entered the classroom, appeared in anthologies, and was treated by scholars in critical studies. This book follows in this tradition, as science fiction meets with another highly popular cultural form that has gradually come to merit critical study: rock music.

Rock Heroes and Mythical Personas

Rock music asserts vitality. It also tends to resist conventionality. In several Rush songs, for example, Geddy Lee, the singer, is given lyrics by the band's lyricist and drummer, Neil Peart, that make assertions against a system that would deny a person's vitality. In one of their signature songs, "Freewill" (1980), he declares that he will assert his free will. For, as the Danish philosopher Søren Kierkegaard wrote in *Either/Or*, if one chooses not to decide one has already made a decision.

Rock performers play out personas; they engage in contrivance and their rock performances build upon artifice. At times, a listener may hear in the music a sense of conflict as the vocalist battles the mysterious forces that assault him. These tensions and dramatic conflicts are at the root of stories. The form of the fable is utilized to bring listeners to fabulous worlds. This fable veers away from traditional realism, often into fantastic places. Sometimes it explores a world of mystery with dark humor. The contemporary fable is a story at play; it is the enjoyment of story for its own sake, observes Robert Scholes. Meanwhile, the dark contemporary fable stares out into the wasteland with a recognition that may remind us of the satire of Jonathan Swift or Voltaire.[5]

The lead singer of a band, the rock music front man, is a mythical figure. That very visible figure onstage has at times been likened to a shamanic figure who casts spells. The singer enters the music and energizes an audience. The mythological potency of such performers can be examined through reference to symbolic rituals. These symbolic rituals have been investigated by Mircea Eliade (1907–1986), a Romanian mythologist and scholar of comparative religions. Eliade produced an important study of shamanism and numerous inquiries into ritual, myth, and symbols. He also wrote novels such as *The Forbidden Forest*, which presented an escape into mythical time. Along with Carl Jung and Joseph Campbell, he was one of the significant expositors of myth in the twentieth century. Eliade might see the glam-space rock David Bowie as a shamanic figure, dressed in spandex and makeup, shapeshifting across the boundaries of identity. When Iron Maiden's front man Bruce Dickinson (or, later, Blaze Bayley) sings bassist Steve Harris's adaptation of "The Rime of the Ancient Mariner" he becomes the haunted mariner who has shot the albatross and is chased eternally by ghostly demons. We find a quest into the unknown in songs like this, the kind of mystery that Eliade interpreted through metaphysics as he reached toward "a certain metaphysical valorization of human existence."[6]

Rock, Science Fiction and Wonder

Rock music is an exercise in wonder. When imaginative science fiction meets with rock music it reminds us of this. Rock music is a form of serious play and innovation, an act of rebellion and liberation. Of course, for rock music's business entrepreneurs rock is a business that sells recordings as commodities. The artists who make the music clearly appreciate the financial rewards of doing so. Rock rebellion gets co-opted, commodified, and sold. However, while the industry is about artifice for profit, for several musicians making music, songwriting, and recording continues to be about discovery and freeing the spirit. Mythology and science fiction motifs have been a feature of their musical exploration and a means for their audiences to explore their own creative capacity for wonder.

Rock music fans revel in that capacity for wonder and celebration of life. They know that rock is exciting and stimulating; it gets into the bloodstream and takes them beyond themselves. If you were to pick up a handful of sand you would be holding about 10,000 grains, Carl Sagan once pointed out. That would be more than the number of stars than we can see with the naked eye.[7] When Bob Dylan wrote "Every Grain of Sand" his song expressed the wonder that he and poets before him, like William Blake, had discovered in the tiniest particles of our world. Blake once wrote: "To see a world in a grain of sand/ And heaven in a wildflower." Similarly, people looking up at the night sky have felt wonder at the sheer magnitude of the reaches of space. Science fiction conveys this wonder and mystery of the cosmos and rock performers and their audiences likewise respond to this sense of awe.

The simple child's song about wondering at a star is amplified when a progressive rock band like Rush, for example, turns to science fiction to express their sense of wonder. They announce defiantly that their imaginative speculations and ambitious music making cannot simply be reduced to pragmatic requirements of a music business that emphasizes the manufacturing of hit singles and the creation of profits. Across more than thirty years, Rush has developed a large fan base. Today they are applauded when they take off on their speculative excursions into science fiction worlds. Yet, when they sing about a dark star, the Greek world of myth lies behind this. Our word "disaster" comes from the Greek meaning "bad star." You can see the word astral there and the "dis" prefix that we find in words like disgust, distraught, disturbed, or dysfunctional. We are thrown back to our connection with the ancient world of myth. Like that ancient Greek audience we too look at the universe with wonder.

Rock Music and the Power of Myth

An adventurous progressive rock song that is filled with mythical imagery is like a musical epic. It is recklessly long, filled with rhythmic shifts in time signature, and it allows for a narrative that can be based in the monomyth. The monomyth is an archetypal plot structure that was engagingly expressed in Joseph Campbell's insights in *The Hero with a Thousand Faces* (1949). It is a story that focuses upon a quest, or a journey, like Iron Maiden's "Run to the Hills" or "Rime of the Ancient Mariner." We find it in dozens of science fiction films. Campbell calls this pattern a single "consciously controlled" sequence that appears in myths and folk tales from all around the world. Called to adventure, the hero takes up the challenge to go on a journey and enters an initiation phase. He or she crosses a threshold into an unfamiliar setting. Then the hero confronts a series of trials. The hero encounters adversaries and obstacles and has to use unique abilities of courage, intelligence, strength, or character and is sometimes assisted by helper figures. The action proceeds to a climactic point at which the hero succeeds, or has a moment of revelation and realizes something. Then our hero returns with gifts for his or her society, which may be increased wisdom, insight, prowess, or strength of character. The hero may confidently venture forth, or be exiled, or tossed into the unfamiliar world.

Along the way there may be monster figures, troublesome terrain, or he may meet a temptress. The return may involve escape from certain doom, a flight from the strange world. In the return the hero finds the strength to push back across the threshold and become part of a change that may come to the society he returns to.[8]

For David Bowie's character Major Tom there is no return to society. Bowie sings the first person story of an astronaut who leaves his tin can of a spaceship to take a walk in space. Upon encountering complications, Major Tom is set adrift and becomes lost in space. In Bowie's song, where the stars are very bright, Major Tom is a doomed traveler.

Usually, the adventure of a hero suggests movement and transition, life-challenging encounters, and transformation. In the heroic quest archetypes are re-enacted. At the core of these archetypes are truths that express our humanity, universal figures which are relevant to all societies. We have seen these archetypes in films. *The Matrix* gives us an oracle, a figure derived from the ancient Greek oracle of Delphi. *Star Wars* unfolds the monomyth and a story of a quest for the father who is a dark figure. We are reminded that in our world of technological change the ancient and the primal is still with us. One cannot simply let go of the past. It lingers in the present.

The power of myth, as Joseph Campbell observed, is very much still with us. In Robert Silverberg's "After the Myths Went Home," a society believes that it can do without myth. Figures of myth are reincarnated through a time machine. But then the myths are put away and banished. Consequently, the society no longer has mystery or heroism. Like that society, we are sometimes forgetful of mythic power. A realistic and pragmatic world claims that myths are just stories. Yet, myths, from time immemorial, have always been a form of inquiry, a way to transmit values. "The world is too much with us," the poet William Wordsworth once lamented. "Getting and spending we lay waste out powers/ Little we see in nature that is ours/ We have given it away/ a sordid boon." Wordsworth's poem ends with the narrator's claim that he could be "suckled in a creed outworn" if only he could have the vision to see Proteus rising from the sea or hear Triton blow his wreathed horn. The surface of a world of commerce, labor, and business as usual is a world that hides the power of myth; it is a world that would call myth "not true." However, that perspective is one of a naïve realism that neglects other dimensions of human experience.

The rock performers who are discussed here revive mystery and the heroic in their songs, albums, and performances. They reanimate the world by returning mythological energy to our social imagination and discourse. The uses of enchantment, as psychologist Bruno Bettelheim once observed, bring new energy to life. What the rock musicians discussed here affirm is the power of story, the vitality of creative imagery, and the dynamic engagement of music with the human spirit. When rock turns to science fiction, or to myth, it is drawing upon deep psychic sources of imagery that are among the most potent collective resources of the human race.

Musical Creativity and the Myth of Dionysius

In 1969, the same year that David Bowie recorded "Space Oddity," the United States space program launched the Apollo rocket toward the moon. In Greek mythology Apollo was "the shining one," a god of light and sun, a god of rational order and symmetry. His curious counterpart was Dionysius. Whereas Apollo was neat and orderly, Dionysius was passionate and messy. Dionysius was the god of wine and revelry, earth, underground power and fertility: a god of intoxication. The philosopher Friedrich Nietzsche, in *The Birth of Tragedy from the Spirit of Music*, proposed that art itself was a dynamic interplay between the orderly power of the Apollonian and the destructive and creative chaos and ecstatic energy of the god Dionysius. The song and dance of the barbaric, the primal fire of rock, owes much to the Dionysian. Rock musicians are the progeny, the ancestors, of Dionysian passion.[9]

In the late nineteenth century, Nietzsche argued against the dullness, lack of courage, and mass-minded behavior that he saw around him in the Europe of his own day. He used a myth, the story of Zarathustra, to assert that the values that kept that society so enervated had to be transvalued. In his myth of Zarathustra he argued that a modern man needed to be heroic, like a man walking on a wire across an abyss. Later he said that one needed a will to power: a phrase that has often been misconstrued. Nietzsche meant not power over others but power within one's individuality. That was the uniqueness of the superman, the Übermensch. This idea has found its way into the poses of rock performers. The amplified power of guitars, the muscular energy and tribal pulse of drumming, the shrieking wail of a vocalist all mark the aspiration toward a Dionysian breaking through to transcendence.

Composer Richard Strauss took "Also sprach Zarathustra" as the theme for his powerful musical composition that became the familiar score for *2001: A Space Odyssey*, the science fiction film based upon Arthur C. Clarke's novel. The thunderous percussion and memorable musical motif of that composition was part of the German romantic heritage from which Nietzsche emerged. Nietzsche was deeply drawn to the music-drama of Richard Wagner, which had a strong influence on John Williams's music for *Star Wars*. Nietzsche's interest in music followed closely the philosophy of Arthur Schopenhauer, who posited that music is considered the highest of the arts. In his view, music can provide a moment of release from the inexorable power of the Will which courses through the world. Nietzsche, upon listening to Wagner, wrote to his friend Erwin Rohde: "Every fiber, every nerve twitched; for a long time I haven't had such a long lasting feeling of rapture."[10] Such words might echo the experience of a rock music fan emerging from a concert.

Nietzsche believed that the artist is an individual of rare sensitivity who can listen for the intimations of the world-soul. The musician feels the power of some unseen force and desires to bring this to the world. Nietzsche wrote: "To those real musicians.... Someone who [has] put his ear to the ventricle of the world's Will who [has] felt the raging desire for being a roaring river or as a most sublime creek pouring into all the veins of the world—and who would not immediately break."[11] The metaphor suggests that a stream of energy may flow through the musician. He or she can draw upon a powerful source of creativity or become a vehicle for sublime beauty.

Rock and Romanticism

What rock musicians have in common with Nietzsche, who composed music on piano, is their inheritance of a pose of rebellion against

Introduction

Enlightenment reason. In the 1980s Robert Pattison linked rock music with romanticism, which, in its English and German forms, countered an emphasis upon rationality with the reminder that we are also emotional, intuitive, feeling beings. Pattison called rock music "the triumph of vulgarity" and contended that rock refuses to submit to measures of good taste. He recognized "various Romantic myths of which rock is composed" and considered rock as a world of thought. The London based music critic Simon Frith, in his review of Pattison's book, *The Triumph of Vulgarity*, pointed out some of the shortcomings of this view. The romantic myths largely resided in what he called the "art school bands": the Rolling Stones, the Yardbirds, the Who, Cream and Led Zeppelin. (Eric Clapton, Jimmy Page, Pete Townshend, and Keith Richards all attended art school at one time. John Lennon did also.) Frith argued that Pattison's thesis that rock was black music, or the blues, meeting with white Romanticism failed to account for bohemian influences and sources of rock. Meanwhile, as a reviewer in *The Nation* (March 28, 1987) pointed out, in commenting upon rock music we cannot only "resituate [rock songs] on a high cultural terrain" in terms of traditional musicology. Our approaches have to be more varied. Rock is more than "an organic development of Western Romanticism expressed in the vulgar mode," as Pattison pointed out. Indeed, rock is this, in part, but it is also something more.[12]

The chapters that follow propose that the creations of science fiction are another way to look at rock's quest for freedom, wonder, and ecstasy. Certainly, the German romanticism of Novalis, Hoffmann, Holderlin, or Nietzsche and the British romanticism of Coleridge, Blake, and Shelley are precursors for the rock attitude that music is liberating, that imagination is to be celebrated, and that rebellion against confining norms is imperative. These poets and thinkers all sought to proclaim the power of imagination and dwelled in dark fantasies. They turned to the force of poetry and story. Rock music, likewise, in our age of science and technology, has combined these impulses with the imaginative resources of science fiction. Transcendence, which was so important to the romantics, is a feature of the science fiction genre. It is a significant feature of rock music as well. The choice to use science fiction motifs and concepts is an assertion of creativity. It provides a dream-world, a speculative wonder-world, or a way of critiquing present day assumptions about what is "real." It offers a way of storytelling and image-making that stretches the musical and visual imaginations of rock music listeners.

Listening to the Rock Universe

You and I are involved in what we listen to. You have your own unique way of listening, the way that you respond to different songs and rock performances. Your way of interpreting the songs and bands that follow may be different than mine. Two people listening to the same recording of music may hear it differently. Their perception of the same music event is different.

Imagine that the astronomers Johannes Kepler and Tycho Brahe are gazing up at the dawn. As the moments of dawn unfold, they look out at the horizon in the same direction. Surely, the distance between the horizon and the sun is increasing. However, they see different aspects of the same reality. Kepler, attuned to the Copernican theory of the universe, recognizes that the earth is in motion. Tycho, still holding to the Ptolemaic view that the solar system moves around the earth, sees the sun rising and in motion. Their interpretations of the same phenomena each reflect a way of seeing. That is just as true when we hear a rock music recording.[13] We are all individual listeners with our own interpretations.

The range of sound that a listener hears may be compared with the spectrum of light. That spectrum of light is the mix of the component parts of the white light of the sun. Isaac Newton, in 1666, cut a small hole in the shade by his window to let in a point of the daylight from the sun. He placed a prism between the light and the far wall of his room. Then he could see that the sunlight had dispersed into a spectrum of light. Like Isaac Newton, we see the phenomenon of light. When the refraction of light gives us a rainbow in the sky, this suggests to us that the spectrum of light is objectively there in nature. Yet, that phenomenon needs a beholder, a way of seeing. Likewise, there are thousands of recordings available around us but a recording needs a listener. When the MP3 or CD plays, or when a needle falls onto the turning LP vinyl record, those sounds come to us. How we listen in that moment is crucial to our experience of the music. Recordings need you, the listener, to engage your own interpretations.

A sound recording holds an act of the past, a voice that is caught in time, one that has been captured for posterity. Musicians know that music itself is restless and full of change. Music is heard by the man who stands on a platform, iPod in hand and earplugs in his ears, watching a train race by. It plays in his mind as he sees a woman on the train looking out. Her speed in time is relative to the man on the platform, as Einstein once pointed out.[14] His iPod plays Pink Floyd's clocks ticking into "Time." Her smartphone is playing futuristic rock. Do they hear the future? Does Rush's Geddy Lee's high tenor cut through the roar of the train to visions of Cygnus or the future of the earth? Does David Bowie's Major Tom imagine a tomorrow before that umbilical cord to his spaceship is cut and he drifts into space? What will rock music continue to borrow from science fiction? This book is about rock and roll memory. It is also about the future. And if the imaginings of rock music are any indication, what an incredible future that will be!

ONE

Rock Music and the Mythic Imagination

Rock bands play with fantasy. The power of myth resonates in their music, their images, and their performances. Rock has reached to Egyptian, Babylonian, Tibetan, and Norse imagery to create imaginative worlds. Haunting suggestions of the Underworld surface in stage spectacles, in song lyrics, and in the imagery created by Alice Cooper, Black Sabbath, Iron Maiden, Kiss, Nine Inch Nails and dozens of other bands. Mythology is recalled in many rock song titles. The Greek hero Achilles is mentioned in Led Zeppelin's "Achilles Last Stand" and in "Cry of Achilles" by Alter Bridge. Cream sings of "Tales of Brave Ulysses." Procol Harum opens "Pandora's Box" and Sinead O'Connor sings "Troy." Trivium is torn between "Scylla and Carybdis." Judas Priest turns to Nordic myth for "Halls of Valhalla" and Asia sings "Valkyrie." Dionysius lingers behind Third Eye Blind's song "God of Wine."

Rock music exercises wild imagination. It tears through convention, rebels against the commonplace, and conjures up figures from beyond the earth. Science fiction and myth cross rock genres: they appear in the shifting guises of David Bowie and in the progressive rock of Yes and Emerson, Lake and Palmer. They come onstage in the space-age stage shows of Parliament and George Clinton's funk. Medieval imagery abounds in heavy metal and hard rock, including in songs like "Neon Knights" by Black Sabbath and "Stonehenge" by Spinal Tap. Led Zeppelin sings of wonder in "Stairway to Heaven" and gestures toward the exotic, the mystical, and the occult with songs like "Kashmir." The album cover for Led Zeppelin's *Houses of the Holy* recalls

Arthur C. Clarke's *Childhood's End*. The wonders of mythology underlie *Led Zeppelin IV* which bears four symbols that represent the members of the band, symbols that have been traced to Egyptian, Celtic, Rosicrucian, Pagan and Wiccan symbolism.[1]

Myth, science fiction, and cosmic reflection have been a familiar feature of psychedelic and progressive bands. Psychedelia emerged in the late 1960s and brought key and time signature changes, modal melodies, surreal lyrics, and extended instrumental solos. The music accompanied a culture, in San Francisco and elsewhere, that embraced marijuana, peyote, mescaline, and LSD. The music intersected with notions of mind expansion and the thought emerging from figures like Timothy Leary, Alan Watts, Aldous Huxley, and Eastern sages like Paramahansa Yogananda. In America, psychedelia emerged in the music of the Jefferson Airplane, the Jimi Hendrix Experience, the Doors, and Santana. Psychedelia influenced the sounds of Pink Floyd, the Yardbirds, Traffic, and Soft Machine. These artists influenced other bands like the Moody Blues, who are sometimes considered one of the precursors of progressive rock. Psychedelia began to unravel and diminish around 1970 but it would influence many rock genres, including progressive rock, glam, and heavy metal.

The Moody Blues

Pop music met classical music and reflections on the cosmos in the creations of The Moody Blues, particularly on their *Days of Future Passed* (1967) album. On that recording the Moody Blues brought together British pop music and vocal harmonies with the range of a classical orchestra. Mike Pinder and Ray Thomas were central to the founding of the Moody Blues in 1964. The Moody Blues first single was "Go Now," which became a hit in 1964. Like the Beatles, they had been playing in Hamburg, Germany. The group's name emerged from Mike Pinder's recollection of Duke Ellington's "Mood Indigo," which he had heard as a child. They were playing the blues. Mitchells and Butlers (M&B), a brewery, owned many of the clubs in Birmingham. They hoped that M&B might fund them and get them onto the circuit.[2]

With a rich vocal sound and song titles that spoke of dreams, Mike Pinder, Ray Thomas, and Graeme Edge extended their music toward classical orchestration. They were joined by John Lodge and Justin Hayward in 1966 when Denny Laine left the band. Lodge was an engineering student in Birmingham at the College of Advanced Technology. Pinder helped to choose Justin Hayward, from Swindon, England, to replace Laine.[3] John Lodge and Justin Hayward created many of the group's most memorable songs.

The Moody Blues were an influence upon what has been called art rock, or progressive rock. Their song cycle in *Days of Future Passed*, emerging from reflection upon Antonin Dvorak's *New World Symphony*, became one of the first concept albums. The album included the Justin Hayward songs "Nights in White Satin" and "Tuesday Afternoon," which have become staples of classic rock radio airplay. Central to the album are Peter Knight's orchestral arrangements. Graeme Edge's opening and closing poems are recited by Mike Pinder, who composed "The Sun Set" and "Dawn Is a Feeling." The Moody Blues recorded with a symphony orchestra on *Days of Future Passed* (1967). The album cover featured a surreal abstract design.

The Moody Blues followed *Days of Future Passed* with *In Search of the Lost Chord* (1968). Among the songs on the album was Ray Thomas's contribution of "Legend of a Mind," a tribute to Timothy Leary which included Thomas's flute solo. They next produced *On the Threshold of a Dream* (1969), an album mixed in both stereo and quadraphonic. Exploring dreams, this concept album became the band's first #1 album on the British charts and entered the top 20 in America. It includes the group's response to Richard Strauss' "Also sprach Zarathustra," which serves as the theme for the science fiction film *2001*.

To Our Children's Children (1969) was inspired by the first moon landing. With a focus on space travel and children, the Moody Blues created a psychedelic album which included the single "Watching and Waiting." It is an orchestrated recording that is difficult to perform live. The next Moody Blues album, *A Question of Balance* (1970), pulled away from some of this orchestration, but *Every Good Boy Deserves Favour* (1971) returned to it.

The song "Lost in a Lost World" by Mike Pinder begins *Seventh*

Sojourn (1972) on a note of concern about racial tensions and revolution. Justin Hayward sings "New Horizons" of love, hope, dreams, and a quest. There is a lighter moment, with Ray Thomas's vocal on the lilting ballad "For My Lady." The first side closes with John Lodge's vocal on "Isn't Life Strange?" The album served up two successful singles: "Isn't Life Strange?" and the up-tempo hit "I'm Just a Singer (in a Rock and Roll Band)" by John Lodge. The re-release of "Nights in White Satin" also climbed up the charts.

The Moody Blues' world tour ended in 1974, and Mike Pinder left the band. From 1974 to 1978 the Moody Blues were inactive. Then Pinder rejoined them and they recorded *Octave* (1978). During this time, *Days of Future Passed* was taken aboard the spacecraft on the Atlantis Shuttle mission by its chief astronaut, "Hoot" Gibson. The astronaut enjoyed listening to "Nights in White Satin" and "Tuesday Afternoon." Meanwhile, Pinder found the band taking a more pop direction after he left the band in 1978. In an interview, Pinder recalls that he had planned to get together with Jimi Hendrix, but the date turned out to be five days after he died. They had planned to talk "about UFO's and things like that."[4]

Jimi Hendrix

The psychedelic music of the late 1960s served as a bridge to mythical themes, progressive rock, and the phenomenon of space music. Within this movement one of rock's most influential guitarists, Jimi Hendrix, built upon the blues and provided a passionate connection with speculative fiction. In *Jimi Hendrix: A Brother's Story*, Jimi Hendrix younger brother Leon Hendrix recalled his brother's interest in science fiction. They were interested in the Flash Gordon science fiction film serials that played in the activity center nearby in Seattle. Jimi Hendrix liked the actor's name, Buster Crabbe. The brothers liked the films *The Thing* and *The Day the Earth Stood Still*. They wondered where the universe had come from. Jimi Hendrix's cosmic thinking considered the constellations, ice ages, and the planets. Leon engaged in poetry and artwork that reflected an interest in the supernatural. He wrote a poem, "Star Child of the Universe," for his brother. Jimi

Hendrix wrote "Third Stone from the Sun" and "Up from the Skies." He wrote "EXP" with drummer Mitch Mitchell, wondering whether spaceships from distant planets exist.[5]

Hendrix has become almost mythical and legendary. His brilliant guitar playing awaits any listener to his recordings and remastered studio tapes. Turn on a radio or tap into Hendrix on your computer and you are bound to hear his singles: the bluesy "Hey Joe," the psychedelic "Purple Haze," or his treatment of Bob Dylan's apocalyptic "All Along the Watchtower." Dig a little deeper and you will find a thoughtful, speculative mind and an amazing creative gift for improvisation.

Hawkwind

Among the psychedelic bands to play "space music" and promote science fiction themes was Hawkwind. In 1972, Hawkwind performed their *Space Ritual* concert tour with lasers and a light show, costumes, psychedelic imagery, and Stacia, a nude dancer. Hawkwind's *Space Ritual* (1973) was a double album. It was "88 minutes of brain damage," said the ad for the recording. Hawkwind's space rock included Dave Brock's pentatonic scale riffs on guitar. Science fiction writer Michael Moorcock told biographer Ian Abrahams that Hawkwind was "like the mad crew of a long distance spaceship that has forgotten its mission"[6]

Hawkwind may be remembered for their 1972 single "Silver Machine." Dave Brock and Nik Turner of Hawkwind were fans of science fiction and they mentioned science fiction novels and films throughout their work. Brock (b.1941) grew up in Middlesex. Turner, a saxophonist, was born in Oxford. Turner has emphasized the band's interest in providing free music at festivals, such as the 1970 Isle of Wight Festival, during which they played outside the gates.[7] They participated in the first Glastonbury Festival in 1970 and the larger Glastonbury Festival in 1971, which included David Bowie and Traffic. Hawkwind was interactive with their audience, including invitations to their dressing room area after some shows.[8] They improvised extended solos. In his study of progressive rock, Edward Macan criticizes extended soloing by psychedelic bands, calling the long drum solo on Iron Butterfly's "In a Gadda Da Vida" mind-numbing.[9]

Hawkwind's *In Search of Space* (October 1971) made reference to "the ecology thing," according to Turner.[10] Brock's song "We Took the Wrong Steps Years Ago" sounds the warning about actions that have resulted in ecological disaster. "The Watcher" appears on *Doremi Fasol Latido* (November 1972), the band's third album. This is a character from a Marvel comics series who observes humankind from a distance. Lemmy sings above an acoustic guitar accompaniment.

"Sonic Attack" was performed in the *Space Ritual* tour from November 1972. These theatrical concerts were enhanced by a light show. The lyrics for "Sonic Attack" were written by Michael Moorcock and were spoken by Bob Calvert, who called the *Space Ritual* concerts "a mythical approach to what is happening today."[11] Moorcock lived in same area of London as the Hawkwind band members and he performed occasionally with the band.[12] His lyrics for "Black Corridor" on the *Space Ritual* album spoke of space. "Sonic Attack" offered a parody of the "four minute warning" for a nuclear attack, or sonic attack, insisting that listeners ought not to panic. In "Damnation Alley," lyricist Calvert turned to Roger Zelazny's 1971 novel of that title to address a world that has been devastated by nuclear war. A character who is sent to California from Boston fights off monster figures and storms.

"Choose Your Masks," co-written by Moorcock under the pseudonym L. Steele, sets up a situation in which people must choose which mask to wear. One represents chaos and the other represents law. The mask cannot be taken off until the individual is no longer involved in the war. Moorcock also writes "Note from a Cold Planet," a lyric that tells of people who survive in a world that is frozen. They live beneath the earth's surface and have to excavate through the ice to get firewood and to gather familiar supermarket brand items.

"The War I Survived" on the *Xenon Codex* album (1988) makes reference to "slaughterhouse five," suggesting Kurt Vonnegut's novel of the bombing of Dresden in the Second World War.[13]

Myth, Fantasy and Progressive Rock

Mythology and fantasy are closely connected with progressive rock. Edward Macan observes that "many of progressive rock's most representative lyrics draw on mythology, fantasy literature, science fiction."[14] Progressive rock is associated with the development of psychedelic music and space music. We find in progressive rock's various styles rock instrumental solo sections, the use of multitracking, reverb, echo, feedback, and ornate melody lines. With Pink Floyd, in the mid- to late 1960s, emerged the first wave of psychedelic rock. The Moody Blues may also be said to be part of the first wave of psychedelic rock. Their *Days of Future Passed* included a song cycle that reflected a working man's everyday experience. "The Day Begins" sets this theme for the album. In the Moody Blues' "Lost in a Lost World" by Mike Pinder, people search for an answer and wonder if they will be found by love.[15] Another band that contributed to this era was Procol Harum, with their single "A Whiter Shade of Pale" in 1967. In that song the Hammond organ adds an aura of cathedral-like mystery.

A second wave of progressive rock began to emerge with King Crimson, playing in minor keys, with acoustic and electric guitars and Mellotron, while making use of medieval images. Jethro Tull, Genesis, Yes, Gentle Giant, and Emerson, Lake and Palmer were part of this phase of development. In the 1970s, science fiction ideas and mythological elements appeared in the creative work of many progressive rock artists, also including Yes, the Moody Blues, Todd Rundgen's Utopia, and Nektar.

The progressive rock of the late 1960s and early 1970s has been linked with the counterculture or to hippie culture and "aspirations to a better society."[16] Far more was involved than "assigning a narrative" to the songs, Marianne Tatom Letts reminds us.[17] Edward Macan points to the initial association of progressive rock with psychedelic rock and the correlation between progressive rock and classical music in "continuous use of tone and instrumental virtuosity."[18] Other critics have pointed to the link with psychedelic rock's encouragement of synethesia: to see sounds and textures and colors of tone. LSD experience led to light shows by bands like Pink Floyd. Joe Gannon from the Hornsey College of Art brought his talent to Pink Floyd's stage shows. Extramusical props entered concerts by ELP, Pink Floyd, and Yes. The ELP world tour of 1973 was lavish in this respect. Keith Emerson's keyboards appeared as a massive array of technological gadgetry. When Carl

Palmer played his drums laser lights were synchronized with his solos. Genesis and Yes used fog machines and laser lights. Pink Floyd added props: dry ice and a falling waterfall for "Set Controls for the Heart of the Sun." Progressive rock first drew upon "the hermetic streak in psychedelia," Macan observes. It suggested "hidden meanings" for fans who were "insiders," meanings for which "outsiders would be oblivious."[19]

This visual aspect of concert performances was matched by the fantastic visual images created for LP records. The conceptual progressive rock album has always been enhanced by this imaginative cover art work which has often drawn upon surrealism. Science fiction and fantasy scenes are used frequently. These visuals have been described by Macan as "space scenarios, bizarre, futuristic machinery, or a combination of the two." Emerson Lake and Palmer's covers for *Tarkus* and *Brain Salad Surgery*, he suggests, represent "technology gone awry."[20] Examples of science fiction imagery on vinyl records include William Neal's cover for *Tarkus* and H.R. Giger's cover for *Brain Salad Surgery*. The latter ELP album's theme is human self-awareness and consciousness versus dehumanizing technology.

The Concept Album

Mythical imagery and fantasy concepts have contributed to the extended rock album. Progressive rock bands have often presented adventurous and lengthy compositions, or suites, with an emphasis on expression and theatricality.[21] The concept album can provide the appearance of unity with a subject or theme (*Days of Future Passed*, The Moody Blues, 1968), or a set of characters (*Tommy*, The Who, 1969). At times, entire albums are presented in concert performances. Pink Floyd played through its album *The Wall* in concert and the record can be listened to as a unified whole. Marianne Tatom Letts points out that such an approach as this might fit well with Joseph Campbell's concept of the hero's journey.[22]

The Beatles' *Sgt. Pepper's Lonely Hearts Club Band* (1967) is often seen as one of the pivotal concept albums which initiated the art of creating a thematic album. *Sgt. Pepper* creates the band as a character playing for an audience, which we hear applauding and laughing in delight on the first song. We are next introduced to the character Billy Shears, who claims that he is able to get by because of the assistance of his friends. The visual elements contribute to the notion of a concept album and the cover connects with the songs. The Beatles in colorful costumes become mythical uniformed and mustached characters. It seems that the songs could stand on their own. Yet, no singles were released from the album and this further reinforced the idea of a unified total production. The production of this Beatles album compelled multiple engagements in listening from its audience.[23]

Science fiction motifs and fantasy became pervasive in progressive rock album cover art. Roger Dean's outer space covers for Yes are a key example. On the cover of *Fragile* the earth is fragmenting. On *Yessongs*, issued two years later, there is a corresponding image. Yes offers the observation that they were seeking that "which we cannot wholly grasp; this is the material of myth." Macan writes that "for many, Dean's mythic landscapes became visceral symbols of progressive rock."[24] Other artists contributed their imagery: William Neal was associated with ELP and Paul Whitehead with Genesis. Hipgnosis, an art firm in London, was responsible for many Pink Floyd album covers up to *Animals* (1977). They created covers for Genesis, Renaissance, ELP, and Yes. The Yes album *Close to the Edge* had an inner gatefold landscape. Macan describes this image as stretching across a "foggy abyss": a surrealist landscape surrounded by fog and bordered by the sea. The "Close to the Edge" suite is based upon Hermann Hesse's *Siddhartha* and a spiritual quest for truth. So, the cover painting may suggest enlightenment: a quest across the visual landscape that is a spiritual journey.

In much progressive rock album art there is a juxtaposition of technology and nature. Macan points out that "much of the science fiction imagery depicts technology gone awry."[25] Visual artist Roger Dean presents an idealistic holistic society in "mythological, medieval, and Eastern subject matter." This contrasts with the nightmare totalitarian society we see being resisted in some songs (as in Rush). These opposites play out in the song lyrics. On Storm Thorgerson's cover for Pink Floyd's *Animals* we see a gray sky over London and the Battersea Power Plant coughing up soot as a pig drifts over it. This is factory

London: smoky and dismal, polluted and affected by the Orwellian animal farm of pigs, sheeplike followers, and power dogs.[26]

Rock music like that of Pink Floyd makes use of the fantastic to assert the resources of imagination, the energy of music, theatrical play, and the fusion of the visual and musical arts and performance. Since the mid–1960s rock has frequently employed mythological figures to emphasize this. Indeed, in heavy metal and in progressive rock some of this imagery and symbolism has become cliché. Rock songwriters continue to dig down into the archetypal consciousness: to that realm beneath wakefulness and ordinary reality.

The Quest for Imaginative Worlds

Rock music has often allied itself with science fiction motifs as part of a quest for escape from dullness or repetition: a break from the mundane world as it is. This is rock that stimulates imagination. Progressive rock, which was mostly a British development at first, is sometimes described as an extension of the counterculture. Its appeal to fantasy and myth and its connections with classical music contrast with the power chords, or bar chords played in open fifths, by American and British blues based rock bands like Cream, Deep Purple, or Alice Cooper. Some artists, like the multitalented composer and producer Todd Rundgren, in different phases of his career, have moved across this entire spectrum of rock music. However, most bands tend to be categorized by critics in the blues rock or progressive rock traditions.

In the 1970s album covers began to draw upon science fiction fantasy and surreal motifs. Progressive rock music "emerged in the wake of the counterculture" notes Macan, who remarks that it showed a "fascination with epic subject matter."[27] Brian Stableford argues, "The perceived countercultural links between rock music and science fiction may have been largely illusory."[28] More obvious, he says, are mythopoetic fantasy and the folk music tradition that lay behind much rock in the sixties and seventies. This critic has a valid point. However, there were indeed countercultural connections with progressive rock's attention to myth, imagination, and grandiose visions. Countercultural fascination with epic subject matter and mythopoetic fantasy are linked with some strands of science fiction.[29] The "hippie" subculture declined at the same time as the first wave of progressive rock began to wane in the late 1970s to early 1980s. The phenomenon of mythically based progressive rock and the counterculture may be seen as interconnected.

"Few styles of popular music have generated as much controversy as progressive rock," Edward Macan points out.[30] There was antagonism toward this genre from the rock music press. "Critical response to 1970s progressive rock was often brutal," writes John J. Scheinbaum. "Critics decried the genre's virtuosity, complexity and indebtedness to classical or art music as a betrayal of rock's origins."[31] The rock that has been often favored by rock critics is a minimalist chord-driven music that absorbs and assertively faces the grime of the earth. An alternative to this arose in forms like progressive rock that sought to re-enchant the world. However, claims of the authenticity in blues-rock by Dave Marsh, Simon Frith, and others have become matters of record.

It wasn't mythology or flights of fancy that the rock critics had an argument with. It was the break from the blues by these bands and their incorporation of classical music that the rock critics took issue with. Progressive rock bands may have sought a kind of prestige with their turn toward classical repertoire, as Robert Walser suggests.[32] However, the incorporation of classical style also offered an opportunity for virtuosity and musical expression. The Moody Blues connected their recording of *Days of Future Passed* with the London symphony orchestra in 1967. By 1972, Emerson, Lake, and Palmer began producing *Pictures at an Exhibition*, consciously drawing upon Mussorgsky's work. While Keith Emerson was displaying his musicianship by using classical resources, ELO's cover of Chuck Berry's "Roll Over Beethoven" again offered the advice that Tchaikovsky should be told the news of rock and roll's presence on the scene.

In the early 1970s, progressive rock was comprised mostly of British bands that used technological and sociological themes far more often than spiritual ones. Star Trek's William Shatner commented on this in an interview about his spoken word album *Ponder the Mystery*. "I think that prog rock is the science fiction of rock music," Shatner said.[33]

Emerson, Lake and Palmer

ELP was Keith Emerson (keyboards), Greg Lake (guitar and vocals) Carl Palmer (drums). The trio was a pivotal resource for progressive rock, according to Edward Macan, who meticulously analyzed the group through a musicological lens in *Endless Enigma: A Musical Biography of Emerson Lake and Palmer*. On *Tarkus* and *Brain Salad Surgery*, ELP were the creators of imagined worlds that contrasted the creative possibilities of technology with its dehumanizing downside. Yes, Jethro Tull, King Crimson, Renaissance, Gentle Giant and other bands were their contemporaries: part of the rise of the eclectic mix that has come to be known as progressive rock. In a review of Macan's book, Paul R. Kohl asserted, "The progressive rock movement of the 1970s is one of the most reviled musical genres of all time."[34] However, such a perspective may rest upon the preferences of those few previously mentioned major rock critics for blues-based rock and stripped down three chord songs played with attitude. Prog rock, in contrast, emphasized musicianship and musical virtuosity and made use of fantasy literary genres. The blues tradition relied upon guitars, bass, drums, and sometimes an organ or a harmonica backing a focused, grungy, sometimes seedy vocalist. The first wave of progressive rock, characterized by ELP, made use of obvious displays of technology, banks of amplifiers, and stages filled with synthesizers and vast percussion sets.

Those rock critics—Lester Bangs, Robert Cristgau, and Dave Marsh among them—let it be known that they favored blues-based rock and regarded rock as deriving in a lineal descent from the blues.[35] Marsh insisted that only rock based in the blues was authentic. Lester Bangs preferred the Velvet Underground, the Stooges, and the New York Dolls to complex keyboard figures by Keith Emerson, or the vocals of Jon Anderson and the musicianship of Chris Squire, Steve Howe, Bill Bruford, and Rick Wakeman of Yes. For some listeners, there was a vast gulf between Iggy Pop and the MC5, on the one hand, and the guitar pyrotechnics of Robert Fripp of King Crimson or Renaissance's Annie Haslam's three octave vocal range, on the other. Macan argues for a place for progressive rock's fusion of classical music and rock music and its appeal to mythological imagery.

Emerson, Lake, and Palmer were at the center of progressive rock's merging of science fiction themes and images of the fantastic. Their innovative music made use of complex guitar and keyboard runs, shifting time signatures, and the Moog or other synthesizers. Their album *Tarkus* (1971) included a 21-minute piece about fighting a war in the future. The album cover portrayed an armadillo and a First World War tank. The armadillo-like Tarkus, a cybernetic force, battles with Manticore, a mythical creature that is said to represent the counterculture and an idea of naturalness. This, Macan notes, represents a conflict between materialistic and mystic/Gnostic worldviews."[36] Macan argues that progressive rock's use of science fiction and fantasy was an extension of the hippie ethos of the late sixties that supported this argument against the system. (Kohl, in response, asserts that the merger of rock and classical music was an incompatible hybrid.) Macan points to Keith Emerson's interest in the music of Bela Bartok and the music of Alberto Ginastera. He asserts that ELP, employing the synthesizer and making it central to their sound, "were more responsible than any other band for shaping the progressive style."[37] They made "a truly idiosyncratic use of classical forms and techniques in a rock context."[38]

ELP's *Brain Salad Surgery* (1973) included "Karn Evil 9," concerning the earth's process from an ice age to the time of a future war that involved computers and humans. While this widely circulated record made a mark commercially, there was some critical resistance to this album. ELP's most notable recording, *Pictures at an Exhibition*, does not involve science fiction or fantasy themes. It underscores ELP's merger of classical and rock music. ELP brought vast technological stage sets from city to city for the concert tours that accompanied these albums. The rock critics decried this also.

Soft Machine's bassist, Hugh Hopper, saw the "rise of the keyboardist at the center" of progressive rock.[39] The keyboard player often substituted for piano, strings, and orchestra the Moog, the Mellotron, and the synthesizer. Robert Moog had developed the large Moog, which was adapted for the stage into a mini-Moog. The synthesizer followed, with its simulation of strings, horns, and guitar. The synthesizer is an electronic instrument that can be engaged in sound synthesis. RCA Victor created tone generators in the late 1950s. The synthesizer was further developed with the Moog and with the use of sequencers. Robert Moog and Donald Buchla created synthesizer manufacturing companies in 1966. They were soon followed by the Tonus firm and by EMS London. Synthesizers became portable and in the 1970s the synthesizer developed device control with a microcomputer. This was followed in the 1980s by digital techniques.

The incorporation of classical music figures on the keyboard made some of rock's guitar based blues fans upset. Keyboardists drew upon Bach, Liszt and Chopin and borrowed techniques from Bartok, Ravel, and Debussy. Audiences became familiar with Matthew Fisher's Hammond organ solo on Procol Harum's "A Whiter Shade of Pale" (1967). Harpsichord entered the Moody Blues' *In Search of the Lost Chord* (1968) and Procol Harum's "In Held Twas I" (1968). In the early 1970s, Keith Emerson sent his Hammond organ sound through a Marshall amplifier. He made use of J.S. Bach's Tocatta and Fugue in D minor for his organ solo in "Rondo." The rondo form is a basic form of classical music. The rondo has multiple sections. One of these sections, often the first, carries the tonic key. This tonic key section is contrasted with other sections, or episodes. (For example, ABACA.) There may be further complexities in this scheme. These sections introduce other tonal colors and themes. To many listeners, this just did not seem to be rock and roll.

Yes

The visual elements surrounding the band Yes's musical product reinforced connections with science fiction, myth, and fantasy. Roger Dean's artwork for the Yes album covers set forth a style for progressive rock imagery.[40] Rick Wakeman of Yes, recalling Roger Dean, said that "he'd become like a sixth member of the band."[41] Dean's visual iconography helped to create messages that linked with Yes's music, lyrics, and performances.

In Yes some folk elements and classical guitar met with "symphonic" progressive rock, complex vocals, keyboard arrangements, and electric guitar leads. This was matched with Roger Dean's album cover artwork on *The Yes Album* and *Fragile* (1971) and *Close to the Edge* (1972). Jon Anderson's soaring vocals were joined by other band members who also sang. Steve Howe and Chris Squire composed much of the music and contributed their musicianship on guitar and bass respectively. The talented Bill Bruford played drums with Yes. He would also make music with King Crimson, Genesis, UK, National Health, and with his own fusion band. Wakeman has noted that the members of Yes were all "technically gifted musicians" and that each individual was "entirely different" from the others.[42] Typically, Wakeman's keyboard skills complemented the tenor voice of Jon Anderson, the stirring drumming of Bill Bruford, and the complex guitar based work of Steve Howe and bassist Chris Squire. He was able to undertake his own musical innovations with *Journey to the Centre of the Earth* as a solo project and his record rose to the top of the album charts.

Mythical journeys like the one suggested by Wakeman's album were common figures in progressive rock in the early 1970s. It was a time period in progressive rock music that included Yes's *Fragile* (1971) and *Close to the Edge* (1972), Jethro Tull's *Aqualung* (1971), Renaissance's *Prologue* (1972), ELP's *Brain Salad Surgery* (1973), and Genesis' *The Lamb Lies Down on Broadway* (1974). In contrast with Yes, Emerson, Lake and Palmer developed their mostly electric style with multikeyboard sounds. Jethro Tull created an eclectic mix of English folk song and rhythm and blues featuring Ian Anderson's flute playing.

In "Starship Trooper" (1970) Yes's Jon Anderson, Chris Squire, and Steve Howe created a dynamic composition that was given vague lyrics by Anderson that reflect his interest in mysticism and space. The title comes from Robert Heinlein's novel but the song lyrics do not correspond in any way with the book. The trooper is an expansive soul who has traveled across the universe. In one sense, the utopian society in Heinlein's story appears to be without racial discrimination or gender discrimination. In another, Johnny Rico learns that military code of duty carries a "controlled violence to enforce orders." The restriction of voting rights to those who have been in government service suggests a repression of democracy. Heinlein's *Starship Troopers* dramatized war and some readers saw in it a subtext that was political. Yes steered away from that controversy.

The song "Starship Trooper" has three parts: Life, Seeker, Disillusion. The opening motif is repeated often in the song's first section. The song is rich with melodic ideas. Steve Howe provides polished guitar playing over vocal harmonies. There is a bass melody by Squire at

1:41, a bridge at 1:51. "Disillusion" begins at 3:16. At 5:36 there is a descending three-note pattern (D to Bb, resolving on G) and the music winds around these three notes. The final section is carried by Anderson's vocals.

With their releases of *Fragile* and *Close to the Edge*, Yes became quite a popular progressive rock band. Like other bands, Yes went through changes in their sound across the next two decades. Bill Martin observed that the album *Talk* (1994) by Yes "took on the feel of science fiction."[43] The use of computers, Digital Performer, and what he calls "futuristic arrangements" reinvented the sound of Yes. Yes's Chris Squire noted the shift to using the new technology of Digital Performer in recording sessions.[44] Yes guitarist Steve Howe, who was so central to the band's earlier sound, did not like the new "futuristic Yes."[45]

Yes has sometimes been associated with classical music. However, most of their musical figures have little to do with classical harmony. They were inventive with their own musical patterns. *The Yes Album* (1971) was built around science fiction concepts and signaled the Yes sound. "Your Move," "Starship Trooper," "Perpetual Change," "Yours Is No Disgrace" became central pieces in the band's repertoire. *Fragile* (1972) incorporated science fiction and fantasy elements. Rick Wakeman's synthesizers, Mellotron, and organ—all quite costly—contributed greatly to their sound. "Roundabout," as an edited piece, became a single that brought Yes widely to public notice. *Close to the Edge* (1972) offered three tracks, with the lengthy "And You and I," "Siberian Khatru," and the side long title track. This became a top five album supported by a long international tour. By the time Yes released *Tales from Topographic Oceans* (1974) they had become popular and critics called this album overindulgent. The album was musically alive and Jon Anderson's lyrics hearkened to Eastern mysticism. The lyrical approach to the four songs was influenced, in part, by Anderson's reading of Swami Paramahansa Yogananda. Anderson looked through *Autobiography of a Yogi* while on tour in Tokyo. Yogananda's name is derived from *maha*, or great and *ananda*, or bliss. Anderson, on his spiritual search, knowing little about Hinduism, developed a cosmology and made a unique contribution. The album attempts to represent four interlocking *shastras* and to suggest a path to inner peace.

A few years later, Yes developed *Relayer* (1974). The band was now out of critical favor but remained popular. This recording alternates dense instrumental sections with vocal/chorale sections. Some critics wanted songs. The band was composing suites. They were also engaging in side projects. *Olias of Sunhillow* (1976) was Jon Anderson's concept album. His song "Sound Out the Galleon" expressed a fantasy in which an alien race is forced to abandon their planet and find another. The spaceship is the Moorglade Mover, operated by Olias. The album reflects Anderson's speculations in science fiction and his acquaintance with Eastern mysticism. Rick Wakeman created his album titled *Six Wives of Henry VIII* (1973) and *Journey to the Center of the Earth* (1974). Then he produced *The Myths and Legends of King Arthur and his Knights of the Round Table* (1975). For Yes's recording *Going for One* (1977) Wakeman returned to the band after a two year hiatus of reflection and rehabilitation. The content of this album was mystical and abstract on five songs. They were melodic, filled with Steve Howe's guitar work and with the band's vocal harmonies. Rick Wakeman played the organ at St. Martin's Church in Vevey, Switzerland. Their follow-up album, *Drama*, shifted the sound to harder rock. Howe played more electric guitar. John Anderson and Rick Wakeman were missing. Geoffrey Downes and Steve Howe joined the band they called Asia. Yes unraveled.

Jon Anderson continued to explore mythology. He incorporated neo-pagan elements into his lyrics and appears to have sought to express a sense of "presence" in nature: a pantheism and polytheism. His words "gravitate to ancient symbols and ancient myths," Margot Adler has observed. Jennifer Rycenga notes: "They are reclaiming these sources, transforming them into something new and adding to them the visions of writers of science fiction and fantasy."[46]

Klaatu and Nektar

Klaatu and Nektar were creative bands with big dreams and limited followings. Both bands created music that they connected with science fiction and space rock. Klaatu was formed in 1973 in Toronto by John Woloshuck and Dee Long and was named after the character Michael Rennie (and later Keanu Reeves) portrayed in the film *The*

Day the Earth Stood Still. The band later added Terry Draper on drums and Klaatu worked as a trio. They started recording in January 1973. Their work went on periodically for 2½ years. They decided to remain anonymous and let the music speak for itself. At first they did not do public relations bios or appear in public concerts. Their first album *3:47 EST* (named *Klaatu* in the United States) has been re-mastered by Peter J. Moore with Terry Brown sitting in. Drummer Terry Draper took the lead in starting their independent record company. Stephen Peeples interviewed them for promotion for the *Endangered Species* album. They listened often to King Crimson. The Beatles and ELO are cited as influences. (Jeff Lynne's songwriting and production with ELO is clearly Beatles influenced.) A Washington radio program director, Dwight Douglas at WWDC, came close to identifying their names. They were preparing their *Hope* album. Ted Jones provided the artwork for the album covers. The cover for *Endangered Species* appeared like *National Geographic* meets Audubon. When seeking a possible single, Terry Draper suggested writing about outer space rather than about love. "Dog Star" emerged with Hendrix influenced spacey guitar and feedback. They commented that they wanted to avoid the CSN preach to the crowd about save the whales, feeling that that was too sixties.

The progressive rock band Nektar produced several science fiction related titles. Nektar was Allan "Taff" Freeman on keyboards, Derek "Mo" Moore on bass, Ron Howden on drums, and Roye Albrighton, guitar/vocals, who left the band and was replaced by Dave Nelson on guitar/vocals. Mick Brockett provided an array of special effects and the lighting for the band's shows. *Remember the Future* (1973) told the story of a blind boy who communicates with an extra-terrestrial. The melodic progressive rock sound of Nektar on this album reached the top twenty. *Down to Earth* (1974) followed with a circus theme. It included the song "Astral Man." *Recycled* (1975) was Nektar's next release. It is a record that has been described as having a sound similar to that of the progressive band Gentle Giant. *Magic Is a Child* (1977) followed with the use of Norse mythology and the theme of magic. Nektar concluded the decade by preparing the songs for *Man in the Moon* (1980). The link between Nektar's progressive rock sound and science fiction imagination came through clearly in many of their titles for songs and instrumentals: "Astronaut's Nightmare," "Time Machine,"

"Void of Vision," "Desolation Valley," "Automation Horrorscope," "Man in the Moon," "Journey to the Centre of the Eye," "Cybernetic Consumption," "A Tab in the Ocean."

Space Rock-Glam: Todd Rundgren and Utopia

Todd Rundgren emerged as a creative force in recording in the early 1970s following his work with the Philadelphia group the Nazz. He came to public attention with his pop singles "I Saw the Light" and "Hello It's Me." A versatile musician, Rundgren combined creativity and virtuosity with comic satire and the skepticism of a scientist. He had soaked in the sounds of Gamble and Huff and Philadelphia groups and the musical figures of the Beatles and British Invasion bands. He was a fine guitar player, an innovative keyboard player, and an extraordinary background singer for his own vocals. He was also keenly aware of the of the New York rock scene that followed in the footsteps of the Velvet Underground. Patti Smith, soon to be instrumental in the new wave emerging from Max's Kansas City and CBGB's in lower Manhattan, was one of the rock music writers who praised his work. As Rundgen attended to the progressive sounds of Frank Zappa, Yes, John McLaughlin and others, he took on projects as a producer for the provocative New York Dolls, Badfinger, Grand Funk, and other artists. He developed his double-album *Something/Anything?* and his cosmic-tinged *A Wizard, a True Star*.

In this phase Todd Rundgren was perhaps more cosmic than mythological. He recognized the influence of David Bowie during the period when he was assembling and developing the music of his band Utopia. When Daryl Hall commented on Bowie's influence to Paul Myers he called the Bowie influence "all pervasive" and observed that while they did not imitate the music, they copied "the attitude."[47] Bowie had begun exploring his glam phase and orientation that led to his creation of the Ziggy Stardust character and his flirtations with science fiction based transformations.

Todd Rundgren's *Utopia*, released on November 9, 1974, was the product of Rundgren's musical explorations with Ralph Schukett, drummer Kevin Ellmann, Moogy Klingman, and John Siegler. "Utopia

Theme" was written by Rundgren and Dave Mason. While Rundgren was always at the center of the group, band members contributed their musical compositions and creativity to the overall output of Utopia. The space rock-glam phase included a stage show in which they wore spacesuits modified from welder's apparatus with visors. "International Feel" was sung by Rundgren in a space suit in 2009. Following *Faithful*, Rundgren and the musicians from Utopia (John Siegler, Roger Powell, and John "Willie" Wilcox) developed the playful instrumentals for *Disco Jets*. This was a comic parody, a response to then-current trends like *Star Wars*, CB radio, and disco and Rundgren's recasting of the *Star Trek* theme.[48]

Queen

The conspicuously operatic vocals of Queen combined with science fiction themes on their album *A Night at the Opera* (1975). It was a sure recipe for pop music magic. Freddie Mercury's vocals rested upon the layered guitar work of Brian May and were surrounded by the band's rich background harmonies. With those operatic vocals, Queen's *A Night at the Opera* offers a narrative of explorers in space: characters that set off and reach a new world. Upon their return only one year has gone by for them but a hundred years have passed.

The band's first album, *Queen* (1973), reflects the progressive rock of the period. *Queen II* (1974), containing fantasy themes and virtuoso musicianship, reached number five on the British album charts. It featured the single "The Seven Seas of Rhye" and the six-minute "The March of the Black Queen." *Sheer Heart Attack* (1974) showed experimentation with hard rock, heavy metal, ballads, and the English music hall tradition. The single "Killer Queen" suggested the layered music and vocal sound that would appear on their next recording. *A Night at the Opera* launched one of the most successful pop rock bands of its day. It contained the hit "Bohemian Rhapsody" (1977). *News of the World* contained the anthems "We Will Rock You" and "We Are the Champions."

Mythology and astrology underlie the Queen logo, designed by Freddie Mercury. The logo includes the zodiac signs for the four band members: two lions for Leo (Deacon and Taylor), a crab for Cancer (May) and two fairies for Virgo (Mercury). The lions wrap around the Q. The fairies lie beneath one of the lions and the crab sits above Q. A Phoenix rises above this. The design appears to represent the royal coat of arms of the United Kingdom, as much as the band it designates.

Much more than time was lost for Brian May of Queen when Freddie Mercury died and the world came toppling down for him. He retired from music for a while to get his life together and then returned to Imperial College to complete a Ph.D. in astrophysics. Before Queen was formed and shot up the charts he had been in Jim Ring's astrophysics group at Imperial College (1970–74). Physics lived alongside music for many years for May. Earlier, while at the university, he was playing in a band called Smile with Roger Taylor (1968–1970). They formed Queen with Freddie Mercury. John Deacon was soon added on bass guitar.[49] May let go of his focus on physics to work intensely with the band.

May is best known for his fluent and creative guitar playing and the precise guitar solos he has brought to Queen. His guitar sound is layered and has a distinctive tone. Brian May frequently plays a home built guitar, the Red Special. He sang the bass parts on "Bohemian Rhapsody." He is also a living example of a musician who has a deeply developed sense of the correlation between music and mathematics. His knowledge of sound waves, timing and distance contributed to studio work with Queen, such as on the clapping sequence on "We Will Rock You." The stomps were based upon prime numbers and "repeats at various distances." The use of delay created the effect of sounding as if many people were involved in the clap and stomp sequence.[50] May reflected upon the possibility of uniting the audience and developed the rhythmic ideas. The band worked this out in an old London church. This became an audience participation part of their shows, breaking down the distance between band on stage and the audience. Unexpectedly, it became a rousing pulse to build crowd enthusiasm in sports contests and is heard today in stadiums throughout the world.

May's academic work was on hold for the two decades that he was involved with Queen. He returned after 2000 to complete his degree in 2007. May's dissertation inquired into interplanetary dust. This has been described as "a survey of radial velocities in the zodiacal dust cloud."[51] The earth moves through this dust and he wanted to figure out the motion of the dust. Does this dust have anything to do with the origin of the solar system? His website brings together music and astrophysics. *The Guardian* noted May's discussion of "hyperbolic orbits or interstellar particles."[52] Brian May became chancellor at Liverpool John Moores University from 2008 to 2013. This was primarily a ceremonial role, noted *The Guardian*. Yet, the university is also a key site of ground-based robotic telescopes that are trained upon the stars. He has supported the John Moores University's Astrophysics Research Centre. He is an animal rights activist and is interested in photography. May also collaborated with the New Horizons Pluto mission.

Dark Imagery and Heavy Metal

Heavy metal makes use of myth and dark fantasy and it draws upon the horror genre. Bands have created albums with titles like *Demons and Wizards* (Uriah Heep 1972). They have worn tattoos depicting dragons and demonic figures and engaged in escapism and fantasy. Some bands have represented chaos and danger, suggested dark magic or occultism, or insisted upon the haunting imagery of snakes and daggers. Iron Maiden, for example, has drawn upon imagery that has ranged from dynamic mythical heroism and science fiction to gothic horror. Their public presence is filled with British cultural identity and their songs recall Greek mythological figures like the flight of Icarus and Odysseus and the Sirens ("Ghost of the Navigator"). They reference the beast of Revelation and their most familiar image is that of their 'mascot,' the cartoon zombie Eddie.

Metal bands crossing from the subcultural to the commercial draw from settings outside this world. Some appeal to the occult, to the supernatural, or to Norse mythology. Some have names that derive from classical sources: Aeon, Charon, Thanatos, Satirycon. They have addressed mythical forces of devastation. British heavy metal, born in the working class Midlands, seeks re-enchantment while grinding out its assertions against adversity. Black Sabbath and Judas Priest have both sung lyrics about dystopia and songs of concern about the future of the planet earth. The aggressive sounds of heavy metal may channel violence while offering a sense of freedom and catharsis, as Robert Walser and Deena Weinstein have suggested. The symbolism within heavy metal ranges across the fantastic images and sounds of speed metal, death metal, and black metal.

In their studies of heavy metal, Robert Walser and Deena Weinstein have each provided strong and distinctive justifications for the examination of a rock music genre that was rejected by some critics and "reviled" by others. Weinstein offered an insightful sociological approach and Walser set forth a theoretical and methodological approach which has been influential for subsequent investigators of the genre. In his study of heavy metal, Walser pointed to the uses of rock for people who have to come to terms with modernity.[53] Walser wrote that "metal has been ignored or reviled, not only by academics of most stripes, but even by most rock critics."[54] Yet, the fantasy and energy in this medium touches a chord with its core fans. Deena Weinstein argued that metal is the music of the global proletariat.[55] Other voices have joined the conversation. Harris Berger points out that "the world of metal has undergone enormous transformations."[56] Heavy metal has expanded beyond its working class roots. The heavy metal genre provides an array of voices that includes those of both male and female fans. This polyvocality spans the world.

Heavy metal has always "evoked power and potency," notes Walser.[57] Guitar distortion has become a key signifier in heavy metal and hard rock, suggesting power and intensity. Loudness and intensity are coupled with grandiose stances, threatening imagery, and fantasies of power. Terror and death (Anthrax, Poison, Megadeth, Slayer) or evil and blasphemy (Black Sabbath, Judas Priest) express heavy metal transgression. This is heavy metal's mythology. "By 1989 heavy metal accounted for as much as 40 percent of all sound recordings sold in the United States," notes Robert Walser, although "genre boundaries are not solid and clear" today.[58] The term heavy metal itself is contested. For example, Bruce Dickinson would never use it to describe all of Iron Maiden's output. Def Leppard and AC/DC reject the term, while Judas Priest wants to be classified as heavy metal.[59]

Anecdotal accounts suggest that heavy metal fans respond primarily to the sound, fantastic imagery, and energy of the genre. Deena Weinstein makes the observation that heavy metal fans are more inclined to respond to key phrases than to the entire lyric of a song. They listen to the overall sound of the music. The meanings conveyed by the lyrics may be secondary. She tells the story of meeting with Rush fans who knew every word of Rush's "2112" but had varying interpretations of the narrative. The singer of the song is, of course, on the side of the dreamer who found the instrument and does not at all side with the priests. In this song Rush declares their "romantic individualism" against any theocracy that would diminish this. However, not all of the fans who responded to Weinstein's questions about the song saw it that way. Curiously, "narrative was not these fans' strong point," says Weinstein, who explained the story to them.[60]

Of course, the perception of Rush as a heavy metal band might itself be contested by heavy metal fans. Most critics would identify Rush as progressive rock. Weinstein recognizes the variety of heavy metal and notes the fragmentation of metal in the 1980s. She distinguishes between heavy metal and what she refers to as lite metal. Heavy metal remained subversive, rhythmic, driven by power chords. Lite metal combined rock with heavy metal qualities and adapted itself to melodic lines and less heavy bass. With its embrace of romantic themes and MTV it gained radio airplay and a wide audience. Some metal fans would not characterize these bands, like Def Leppard or Bon Jovi, as metal at all. Resisting this trend was speed or thrash metal, in which bands like Metallica rose to prominence. Thrash or speed metal "contrasts with punk's simplicity and nihilism," observes Robert Walser. It brings together heavy metal with punk influences of aggressiveness, critical lyrics, and fast tempos. However, it displays more virtuosity and control.[61] It can be differentiated from the glam metal of Mötley Crüe and Quiet Riot and other bands that have drawn upon the androgyny set forth earlier by the New York Dolls and David Bowie.

Mythology is pervasive in heavy metal. In her sociological study, Weinstein distinguished between two key features of heavy metal: the Dionysian and chaos. Dionysius, the Greek god of wine and revelry, could be both destructive and creative. This was the god of ecstasy, the god of liberation and breaking through into wonder, pleasure, and heightened experience of the moment. Heavy metal seeks this vitality and transcendence. However, it is also characterized by the recognition of chaos, including elements of conflict, confusion, and violence, as

Weinstein points out.[62] The underworld, often viewed as a grotesque realm of apocalyptic horror, is one of its key images. This is an inversion of the sublime, experienced as terror and awe. It is expressed in themes of disorder, defiance, opposition, and destruction. This is a discourse, Weinstein notes, that embodies contradiction and includes images of monsters, the grotesque, mayhem and disaster.[63] With this discourse has come biblical imagery, particularly from *Revelation*, like Iron Maiden's "Number of the Beast." References to the devil connote disorder. Heavy metal also turns to Gothic and horror imagery to denote chaos and turns to sword and sorcery to explore the fantastic.[64]

Heavy metal bands may argue against contemporary forces of destruction, as in Black Sabbath's "War Pigs," or against those of conformity and diminishment of imagination, as Rush does in "2112." They may call for rebellion or change. Or they may simply delight in the imagery of the fantastic, the heroic, or the horrific.[65] Much like Dante once did in expressing the horrors of Inferno, these bands shake things up, challenge the apparent stability of daily life, and they remind us of our vulnerability. Or, like the angels of Milton's *Paradise Lost*, heavy metal offers symbolic rebellion. The dark images of heavy metal may reflect the anxieties and problems of the culture, as critic Robert Palmer has suggested.[66]

Led Zeppelin

Heavy metal's precursors Led Zeppelin and Black Sabbath turned toward what might broadly be called mythology. It is well-known that guitarist Jimmy Page was fascinated with occultism and Aleister Crowley. Page purchased esoteric books, including rare volumes, and he financed the Equinox book shop in Kensington. Led Zeppelin's fourth album includes symbols that are said to represent the four members of the band. Page has said that Led Zeppelin was the alchemy of the elements, a combination of Led Zeppelin's four members. The Hermit from the Tarot on the inner sleeve of *Led Zeppelin IV* has been identified as a variation of the Rider Waite. When asked if he advocates the hermetic tradition, Page has said that he does not advocate anything; he simply hopes that people will find things themselves.[67]

is a romantic figure, raising a microphone like a talisman, strutting among guitar wielding associates and a mad drummer creating fire. The ordinary laws of life are indeed set aside as their song breaks forth with images of ogres, witches, and wondrous cities, bringing us to those places where the mundane world is re-enchanted.

THREE

The Jefferson Starship Takes Off

The San Francisco Scene

Rock music was a crucial resource for the sixties counterculture. Myth and magic came along for the ride. Rock coalesced with lifestyle choices and personal expression. Lengthy hair, bright colored clothing, flowers, beads, jeans, miniskirts, hats, and glasses became sign-systems indicating participation in this relaxation of cultural conventions. Jefferson Airplane was at the center of this movement. They took these signs and turned them into signifiers: images that showed their participation in a mythic, idealized, alternative community. Grace Slick joined vocalist Marty Balin when her band the Great Society dissolved. Paul Kantner and Jorma Kaukonen and Jack Casady soon joined them. They drew upon folk music and the blues and their music unified youthful audiences into a subculture in the San Francisco Haight-Ashbury scene.[1] Jefferson Airplane was the first San Francisco band to sign with a major record label, RCA, and they broke upon the national scene with Grace Slick's plaintive vocals on "Somebody to Love" and "White Rabbit," their drug-culture song recalling *Alice in Wonderland*. Jefferson Airplane was involved with hallucinogens and the quest for alternate lifestyles that brought the counterculture into contact with psychedelic rock. The folklore of the people that J.G. Frazer writes about in *The Golden Bough* (1890) seemed to be at the center of Jefferson Airplane's communal message. The concert became like a sacred rite for the fans of the San Francisco area bands the Jefferson Airplane and the Grateful Dead. In 1970, Jefferson Airplane broke up. Kaukonen and Casady started the blues band Hot Tuna. Paul Kantner's science fiction interlude, *Blows Against the Empire*, launched the band in new directions. Then these musicians reconstituted their musical identity as the Jefferson Starship and evolved into a popular recording group in the 1970s.

Notions of shamanic art were at the center of the explorations of the Jefferson Airplane and the Grateful Dead, as drummer Mickey Hart has pointed out. If we look at J.G. Frazer's second chapter of *The Golden Bough*, we read about the king of sacred rites, or shaman, a role that these bands adopted. Frazer proceeds to specify categories of magic: sympathetic, contagious, or "contact," and homeopathic, or healing. The ethos of the Jefferson Airplane and the Grateful Dead implied that music and community ritual were all of these. In 1967, audiences became entranced by the outpourings of the Jefferson Airplane, the Grateful Dead, and other San Francisco area bands. In the San Francisco scene, rock's base in the working class persisted, particularly in the blues rock stemming from the British invasion bands like the Rolling Stones, the Who, the Kinks, and the Animals. Meanwhile, psychedelic bands like Pink Floyd, Procol Harum, the Moody Blues, and the Nice created a basis for progressive rock between 1966 and 1970. Blues and folk based groups like Jefferson Airplane and the Grateful Dead would continue to foster one brand of hippie consciousness and music, while the emergence of British progressive rock would follow with Emerson, Lake and Palmer, Yes, Genesis, Gentle Giant, Renaissance, and Jethro Tull between 1970 and 1975. The work of Jefferson Airplane is part of this psychedelic phase and exemplifies the musical quest and mythical quest for freedom and transcendence that was vitally present in sixties counterculture.

Jefferson Airplane, in their hallucinogenic, creative outpourings on *Surrealistic Pillow* appeared to be the Dionysian band *par excellence*. Greek mythology speaks of Dionysius, the wine-god, as a force of creativity, destruction, and renewal. In the Greek drama *Antigone*, the Chorus of senators lifts their hands and voices in appeal to Dionysius for healing and transformation for the city of Thebes. Rock music has been linked with the Dionysian by some of its fiercest critics, from Allan Bloom in *The Closing of the American Mind* (1986) to Robert Pattison's *The Triumph of Vulgarity*. Yet, this creative impulse toward breaking free and remaking the world is also one of rock music's strengths. The Dionysian consciousness expresses itself in radical novelty, a willingness to risk ecstasy and chaos. The ancient Greek drama *The Bacchae* by Euripedes warned against having emotion overcome reason. The chorus in *Antigone* indeed appeals to Dionysius as the patron of Thebes but also counsels against humans who dare to exceed the boundaries of moderation.

Rock is immoderate: it seeks highs of ecstasy and wonder and it plays with illusion. Science fiction soon came into the group's songs and album concepts as singer Grace Slick and guitarist Paul Kantner sang about a group of people escaping earth in a hijacked starship in *Blows Against the Empire* (1971), an album nominated for a Hugo Award (but no award was given that year). Kantner imagined spaceships and wrote "Let's Go Together" and Grace Slick opened side two of *Blows Against the Empire* by singing of sunrise, as if of a new age dawning.

The makeup and stage shows of David Bowie and Alice Cooper and dozens of progressive and heavy metal bands are theatrical play and expressions of imagination, Eros, and breaking out of "straight" society. They challenge inherited modes of perception and seek a nonrepressive social order. Play, spontaneity, and fantasy challenge conventional boundaries of order with a kaleidoscopic variety, a sensuous immediacy in which improvisation is allowed to happen. The creative rock band oscillates between work and play, thinking and feeling, fantasy and realism, concept and imagination. It lives within musical structure and ventures to break out musically and sometimes theatrically, wandering into strangeness or tempest and passion. Rock bands often seem to defy order.

Myth and science fiction in the Jefferson Airplane catalog appear to be allied with a search for transcendence. The late 1960s brought a turbulent period of countercultural resistance to the Vietnam War characterized by student protests, calls for change in the social imagination, and drug-induced quests for transcendence. The "sixties," a period that several sociologists suggest extends from about 1965 through the early 1970s, was a time of idealism and socio-political restlessness. The youth culture realized a close connection with rock music. For some listeners, rock music became associated with drugs, sex, spiritualism, or a quest for higher consciousness. With this idealism arose progressive movements in civil rights, feminism, environmentalism, justice and equality, and opposition to war.

Paul Kantner's science fiction recordings suggest a sixties spirit that sought Avalon, an ideal of a mystical place, a new consciousness that would reconstitute society.[2] In effect, the narrators of the songs on Kantner's *Blows Against the Empire* wish to escape, to sail away to create a new world. Theodore Roszak viewed the counterculture as a loose collection of people who felt disaffiliated. Timothy Leary believed that spiritual development could come from LSD and consciousness-raising. Todd Gitlin, observing America through a sociological lens, observed that the counterculture sought pluralism and pursued issues with political resonance and a sense of community free from the mainstream. Science fiction writers veiled social and political concerns in their stories. The vision of some writers, like Paul Kantner, or Michael Moorcock in Britain, fit well with these counter-cultural approaches.

The Jefferson Airplane rose amid a series of cultural symbols that expressed for some people an "anything goes" freedom. Rock supported an ethos of rebellion. It coupled with a negation of convention and "the system." The rock counterculture was never a united, monolithic group. Some of its listeners sought what the counter-cultural attorney Charles Reich, in his book *The Greening of America*, called "Consciousness III." Others fiercely declared their independence and sincerely wished to change the world. They became involved in civil rights, woman's rights, or in social and political concerns. Some rock fans simply enjoyed the music. Evidently, some of the Jefferson Airplane's audience were more interested in listening to music and getting high than in fostering the transformation of society. They protested what they felt to be repressive and then participated in hedonism and expressive indulgence. Indeed, some individuals likely wanted to step out of the society altogether. Others stayed on in their communities, spending time with family and friends, working their jobs, or attending school. Meanwhile, they listened as the Jefferson Airplane pointed toward mythical consciousness and toward new possibilities for the culture. America persisted through the years of the Nixon administration and Watergate, years that saw Woodstock, Altamont, the rise of progressive rock, folk-pop singer-songwriters, and the growing vitality of Motown rhythm and blues.

These were years of change for the Jefferson Airplane, as they morphed into the commercially successful Jefferson Starship.

Blows Against the Empire was an experimental concept album, and Kantner and Slick came up with what they called the Planet Rock and Roll Orchestra. The *Sunfighter* (1971) album followed. Jefferson Starship appeared in 1974. "Miracles" on the *Red Octopus* album was a huge single, reaching number one on the *Billboard* charts. The band's *Earth* (1978) album offered another of their biggest hits, "Count on Me," which reached number eight, and the hit song "Runaway."

In a *Creem* review that began by insulting ELO (Electric Light Orchestra), Jefferson Starship's music was called "faceless, expert and bland."[3] The suggestion in the *Creem* article is that a quality of "seriousness" may be embraced in the lyrics of Bob Dylan, Elvis Costello, Michael Stipe of REM, or in Peter Gabriel and some Neil Young, while one ought to disparage the "vapid" fantasies of other artists. However, the rock of Jefferson Airplane was valued for its relationship with the cultural underground.[4]

Transformation

The years during which some of the members of the Jefferson Airplane reinvented themselves as Jefferson Starship were a time of seeking. Some seekers turned East, quite seriously exploring meditation and spirituality. They pursued alternatives in Eastern religions and theosophy and followed the encouragement of figures like Ram Das (Richard Alpert) to "be here now."[5] Rock musicians like George Harrison, Pete Townshend, and John McLaughlin turned East for Enlightenment. For others, sitars were exotic and talk of chakras was trendy. Esotericism and new age approaches could be co-opted by capitalist entrepreneurs as marketing strategies. Hallucinogenic drugs were tools for a spiritual quest for some people and recreational escape for others. Questioning of authority came with questioning the reliance on technocratic culture and a desire for communal relationship rather than atomization. Many individuals sought peace but had to deal with an often unsuspected undertow of violence present in the counterculture and the wider society. Myth or mythopoetic awareness offered a narrative that was different from conventional daily life in Britain, or in America. Some psychedelic bands, or progressive bands, seized upon these alternatives.

The Jefferson Airplane and other San Francisco bands entered psychedelic music in explorations of human consciousness. Nancy Reid refers to the "maintenance of a healthy mythic imagination."[6] She provides a quote from Jerry Garcia in which he says that when the band gets onstage what they want is "to be transformed from ordinary players into extraordinary ones, like forces of a larger consciousness."[7] The ritual aspect of a Grateful Dead concert was compared by Joseph Campbell to a Dionysian festival. Reid mentions that the band generates "controlled trances" and says: "These shifts in consciousness may be experienced as metaphoric deaths or journeys to a mythic world."[8]

Paul Kantner's turn toward science fiction concepts came during the days that band members were drifting away to other concerns and Jefferson Airplane was dissolving. Kantner had grown up reading science fiction. As a teen, Kantner was fond of C.S. Lewis's *Prelandra* and *Out of the Silent Planet*. He also read novels by Robert Heinlein, like *Methuselah's Children*, which serves as a basis for the story line in his album. (Kantner asked for permission from Heinlein for the use of his images and Heinlein readily agreed.) Kantner developed the project with Grace Slick during a time in which their romance brought pregnancy and a child, China Kantner. The idea of new birth intersects with dreams of a counter-cultural utopia. They will free their child from government and realize a life of freedom. *Blows Against the Empire* was the first recording to make use of the Jefferson Starship name. The record was a silver LP with Russian art on the album cover and a collage inside. The record reached #20 on the *Billboard* album charts.

The transformation of Jefferson Airplane into Jefferson Starship was a gradual process. Paul Kantner's work on his record began after the departure of drummer Spencer Dryden from Jefferson Airplane. Kantner's album was recorded at Pacific High Recording Studios and at Wally Heider's recording studio in San Francisco. Phil Sawyer was the recording engineer. They brought Jack Casady and Joey Covington into the sessions, along with Jorma Kaukonen and Peter Kaukonen, at a time when they were involved with their band Hot Tuna. Also contributing to the recording were members of the Grateful Dead, Jerry

Garcia and Mickey Hart, David Freiberg of Quicksilver Messenger Service, and David Crosby and Graham Nash, who often recorded at Wally Heider's studio. Graham Nash, in his autobiography *Wild Tales*, notes that David Crosby was involved with the Jefferson Airplane members and with Grateful Dead members in a group they called the Planet Earth Rock and Roll Orchestra.[9]

The musical collaborations that developed during this time unfolded in a variety of directions. Crosby, Stills and Kantner wrote "Wooden Ships," which appeared on *Volunteers* (1969). The song was recorded again for *Crosby, Stills and Nash* (1969) and *So Far* (1974). "Wooden Ships" is apocalyptic. After a nuclear war the wooden ships seek shelter. This group would sail away to freedom—not on a spaceship this time. They are leaving and not needed by the culture they will escape from.

Paul Kantner's enthusiasm for science fiction was matched by David Crosby and Graham Nash. David Crosby writes in his autobiography *Long Time Gone* (1988, 2007) that he "soaked up huge amounts of science fiction."[10] He added: "if you want an education, read." Graham Nash mentions reading Ray Bradbury's *The Silver Locusts* while traveling and being held for his papers at the airport by immigration officials in Vancouver.[11] Returning home, he wrote a song on the cover pages of the book. Nash's self-education, however, has primarily been in photography and visual art, Beat poetry, and social-political concerns. He studied the art of M.C. Escher and Expressionist art and he has practiced the art of photography for many years[12] Nash claims that his songs are simple and do not approach the complexities of some of the songs written by Crosby or by Stephen Stills.[13]

Blows Against the Empire

They gathered to produce an improvised free-form rock on songs that were mostly created by Paul Kantner, alone or in collaboration with others. Kantner's acoustic guitar and his banjo playing on his cover of Rosalie Sorrel's "Baby Tree" contributed to the folk music inspired edge of the album. Grace Slick's piano playing served as one of the musical centers for the recording and it seems that her shimmering multi-tracked vocals on her own composition, "Sunrise," took the album to the higher dimension toward which it aspired. The overall theme was one of countercultural idealism typified by a breaking away from the constraints of earth. The power and harmonies that Grace Slick achieved on that song certainly seemed to transcend what one of Shakespeare's characters, Lorenzo, once called "this muddy vesture of decay." Likewise, the vocal harmonies on "Have You Seen the Stars Tonite" are another highlight of the album.

The free-flowing jam quality of the record is a clear match with the freedom sought by this collective. The story line says that they seek to break free of the oppression of Uncle Samuel. "Mau Mau (Amerikon)" begins the album with Kantner's vocal out front and a raggedy proto-grunge sound. There is an admonition to celebrate and play and to come alive. "The Baby Tree" offers a folk song played on banjo that brings us to an imaginary island where the babies grow on trees and fall to earth into the loving arms of happy couples. With "Let's Go Together" the collective joins together in an energetic ensemble that sounds like a live performance. The energy created by acoustic guitars supports characteristic chorus vocals. Kantner's singing is joined by those of others and Grace Slick's voice cuts through on top of them, holding out notes. In "A Child Is Coming" the group gathers before dawn, tripping on acid, wondering at the possibilities of the break of dawn and a new day. Kantner introduces the image of the park and claims that he will be the diplomat there. We hear a guitar chords-driven song with bright lead guitar lines. Slick's vocal rises in the background, echoing the lines sung by Kantner. David Crosby joins his vocal with other vocalists on this song and on "Have You Seen the Stars Tonite" on Side Two. Graham Nash mixed the second side of the *Blows Against the Empire* album, while "acid drenched."[14]

On Side Two, Grace Slick's powerful female vocal almost reshapes the texture of the album, piercing into the sunrise. She sings both vocal parts, overdubbed. "Have You Seen the Stars Tonite" adds to this vocal peak of this record and Kantner's 12-string guitar drones out octaves and fifths in an unusual alternate tuning in open C. Background vocals are overdubbed and processed. Sound effects suggest engines and the starship in flight. There is an inserted audio piece from a George Pal *War of Worlds* film from 1953 in which a woman cries out to get free and get out and a ray gun fires. The sound effects contribute to the narrative which continues on Side Two. Once Grace Slick's vocals take flight on "Sunrise," the song blends into the narrative of "Hijack." The group seizes a transport to the orbiting starship and then ventures off into space. They leave orbit in "Home" and this leads into "Have You Seen the Stars Tonite." The ship's engines are prepared in "X-M." A mutiny is fought for control of the spaceship. The idealists question if they ought to surrender or keep going. The idealists win the struggle. A gravity sling-shot propels the ship around the sun and out of the solar system.

Meanwhile, the band's transition to Jefferson Starship was under way. Vocalist Mary Balin, who had left Jefferson Airplane, would return later to Jefferson Starship and record the hit "Miracles" on *Red Octopus*. Jorma Kaukonen and Jack Cassady formed Hot Tuna. In 1971, *Sunfighter*, was released by Kantner and Slick. It included an ecologically-centered song, "Earth Mother," written by Jack Traylor, who was an English teacher and a friend of Kantner.

Jefferson Starship was more mainstream commercial than Jefferson Airplane. They took off on the *Billboard* charts in 1975. They played a free outdoor concert in New York's Central Park that year, as their *Red Octopus* album was released. That recording, with the hit single "Miracles," became a platinum album, selling thousands of copies. Of course, today you can purchase CDs or downloads of virtually all of the band's commercial output. The *Blows Against the Empire* recording has been remastered and issued with bonus tracks, such as Kantner's seven minute acoustic demo of "Hijack." In 1992, *Tales from the Mothership* emerged as a double-album recorded live at Roswell, New Mexico. The album included musicians Mark Aguilar, Jack Casady, and Papa John Creach. In 2008, *Tree of Liberty* included Jefferson Airplane and Jefferson Starship material. Cathy Richardson provides vocals in the absence of the retired Grace Slick. The new band includes David Frieberg, Danny Baldwin, and Jude Gold, replacing Aguilar.

Starships and Spaceships

The name Jefferson Starship calls to mind one of the iconic images of science fiction: the spaceship. When Jules Verne wrote his science fiction story *From the Earth to the Moon*, about sending space voyagers toward the moon, he indicated that rockets might be propelled by gunpowder. In 1970, NASA scientists anticipated that chemical propulsion rockets could travel at about 40,000 miles per hour. That July, American astronauts Neil Armstrong, Buzz Aldrin, and Michael Collins achieved the successful Apollo mission in which men walked on the moon. However, starships that could reach Alpha Centauri, over four light years away, remained a dream. NASA designed other missions to space, such as the Space Shuttle. There were the failures of the *Challenger* and of the *Columbia*. Satellites were sent into space at greater distances. To reach deeper points in space scientists needed to create ion thruster engines and plasma engines. Even so, these do not have enough propulsion to aim at the stars. To reach even the nearest of the stars would require further designs and a costly expenditure of fuel. Science fiction writer Robert Heinlein once said that if one could surpass 160 kilometers above earth one could extend that more easily to points in space more distant. As physicist Michio Kaku points out, that first 160 kilometers is the most expensive part of a launch, when a rocket ship is pushing upward against gravitational force.[15]

So, is a starship possible? The television series *Star Trek* popularized the idea, beginning in the 1960s. The Starship *Enterprise* was able to achieve warp speed and trace rapidly across space, "the final frontier." The Jefferson Starship imagined possibilities like that. They were a band in the spirit of late sixties revolution, yearning for social transformation. More than pointing toward any kind of technology, the starship idea suggested something cosmic, or the hope of transcendence. At first, this hope for cultural and personal transformation emerged in the context of the Kantner concept album, which was filled with the vision of science fiction.

As an avid reader of science fiction, Kantner knew that the spaceship had become an iconic image throughout the genre. When scientists began addressing the possibilities of rocket propulsion, science fiction writers began to use the image of the rocket frequently. In rock music iconography, the spaceship may be a symbol for launching and taking off, departure from convention and norms, or the aspirations of a band. In Kantner and Slick's science fiction-themed recording they recognized that a spaceship is also a habitat, or something like a house in which a group of like-minded people could travel in search of a new way of life.

The starship could be a universe unto itself. *Star Trek* provided a crew with something like a comfortable middle-class home that was often disrupted by hostile forces in the universe. In the 1950s, James Blish, one of the contributors to that series, wrote a series of novels in which cities of Earth are launched into space by using antigravity devices. Gene Wolfe, in his *Book of the Long Sun* series, has featured a spaceship that carries medieval city-states. Frank Herbert's *Destination: Void* (1966) presents spaceships managed by human brains, or Organic Mental Cores. The story suggests that artificial intelligence may one day operate the spaceships. The spaceship image continues to be familiar in recent fiction, television, and in Oscar nominated films like *The Martian* (2016).

The image of starships repeated throughout the 1970s in popular rock music album cover graphics with the bands Boston and Electric Light Orchestra (ELO). Starships burst into battle in George Lucas's *Star Wars* and carried voyagers to other solar systems in film, television, and science fiction novels. However, NASA was no closer to creating an interstellar rocket. In 2005 the Prometheus nuclear rocket was funded at $430 million but funding was sharply cut to $100 million the next year. Scientists had envisioned a nuclear propelled rocket in the late 1950s into the early 1960s. The Limited Nuclear Test Ban Treaty of 1963 curtailed that. The project ended largely because it was considered too dangerous. The British Interplanetary Society pondered the idea of a nuclear rocket in the 1970s, Project Daedelus, but this remained a speculative exercise filled with technical problems. For a spaceship to "go where no man has gone before" it will have to travel the speed of light. When NASA sends out space probes they may be sent into the orbit of a planet to boost their velocity, observes Michio Kaku. An example is the Voyager spacecraft that was directed toward Neptune. A slingshot effect "whips them around" the planet.[16]

The Jefferson Airplane could easily be constructed as the Jefferson Starship: a musical unit of talented musicians that could extend the creative work that had begun in San Francisco in the 1960s. Building an actual starship is quite another matter. One of the technical problems involved in constructing a starship is the great size of the space vehicle. It has been suggested that nanotechnology could reduce the size of spaceships; they need not be the massive size of a Starship *Enterprise*. However, the image of the large spacecraft persists. Consequently, scientists have proposed that such a project of starship construction should be performed in the weightlessness of outer space. There heavy objects could be lifted and moved far more easily than they ever could be under the weight of gravity. However, building the International Space Station and sending space shuttle launches to assemble it is tremendously costly. Scientists have explored the idea of a "space elevator" as a means to reduce the cost. Science fiction writers Arthur C. Clarke, in the *Fountains of Paradise* (1979), and Robert Heinlein, in *Friday* (1982), introduced the idea, but the idea stalled until about 1999, when NASA reconsidered the idea. As Michio Kaku explains in *Physics of the Impossible* (2008), the reconsideration of the space elevator idea was stimulated by the development of carbon nanotubes by a Japanese chemist, Sumio Iijuma. Lighter but stronger than steel cables, nanotubes can withstand pressure and hold fast a ribbon-like space elevator to transport materials (Kaku 167). However, it remains a technical difficulty to produce nanotubes that are sufficiently lengthy to make this operation successful. Also, as Kaku points out, "microscopic impurities ... could make a long cable problematic" and "atomic scale defects could reduce the strength of the nanotube cable."[17] Meanwhile, because satellites near the earth rotate there would be the potential of collision with the space elevator.

Space travel is further complicated by radiation, shifts in temperature, and weightlessness, which has many impacts upon the human body. This was evident in the recent experience of astronauts who returned to the Earth's atmosphere after having been in space for a year. There is also the matter of time. It would take many years in earth-time to reach distant stars. A single human life would not have the longevity necessary to complete the trip. It would require some form of intergenerational crew that could one day realize the arrival of the mission.

Even so, a rocket may be a bridge between worlds. It may carry passengers from our world into an unknown world. Or, it may bring the alien into our world. Psychologist C.G. Jung compared the spaceship with a mandala. For Jung, a mandala is a mythical figure which holds out the hope of unity; it is an "individuation symbol" or an "archetype that has always expressed order, deliverance, salvation, and wholeness."[18] The rocket and spaceship has been a primary image of American technology since "the new frontier" and space program initiated by John F. Kennedy.[19]

The spaceship of Paul Kantner's design was one of a self-contained society that had developed its own perspective. He dreamed that the break of this spaceship community from the larger society could lead to renewal. Robert Heinlein's *Methusalah's Children* provided the basis for this counter-cultural vision. Heinlein's "Universe" and "Common Sense" appeared in *Astounding* in 1941 and they were reprinted as *Orphans of the Sky* in 1963. The spaceship society that Kantner presented led directly to the Jefferson Starship. They are the spaceship family.

Robert A. Heinlein's story "Universe" provides the theme that a spaceship might carry people forth on a multi-generational mission into space. *Orphans in the Sky* (1963) collected this story with its sequel. Hugh Hoyland and his companion live on a spaceship, an interstellar world in motion, on which many generations have lived and died. A mutant reveals to him the night sky and its stars and planets beyond the spaceship: a universe he has never seen. The story pulls together the pieces of a back story that recalls that there was a mission to a star that was expected to last for sixty years. There was a mutiny and there was a destructive time that wiped out the memory of the mission. From this Kantner drew the theme that a family-like group of companions might escape the socio-cultural limitations of 1960s America and dream of creating new possibilities.

Similarly, Ray Bradbury's *The Martian Chronicles* (1950) has "family rockets." They are sent on leisure adventures to the moon. Of course, Bradbury, like Kantner, was utilizing science fiction to critique his society. In the linked stories of Ray Bradbury's *The Martian Chronicles* humanity is exploring Mars. The Martian population has been destroyed and the planet is being colonized. Meanwhile, the Earth is under the peril of thermonuclear warfare. Bradbury critiques the frontier thesis of historian Frederick Jackson Turner, who asserted in the 1890s that the American frontier had closed. It was the Western frontier that had provided opportunity, Turner theorized. The frontier was pivotal in American history: fostering democratization, encouraging vigor, calling for the transformation of America. In Bradbury's stories, his characters that colonize Mars come to think of themselves as Martians in this new landscape. In "The Million Year Panic" a father promises his children that they will see some real Martians. However, the Martian population has been decimated and when they arrive he points to a canal in which they see their own reflections.

Like Kantner in his songs, Bradbury explored contemporary society through his stories and dealt with social issues that were significant during the time during which he was writing. On Earth, a scarcity of resources prompts international conflict. Transnational corporations have become more powerful than governments. One entrepreneur leaves Earth for Mars and seek financial gain. In "The Offseason," a colonizer opens a hot dog stand on Mars, expecting that more people will come from Earth and make him wealthy by buying his hot dogs. Then he sees the Earth explode in atomic devastation and he knows that he will never see any customers. In "Way in the Middle of the Air" a racist store owner in the American South is annoyed when the African American population flees the area and moves to Mars.

Heinlein's *Methuselah's Children* (1958) shows the departure of a group of families to space so that they can escape the persecutions they experience on earth. (They are thought by the people on earth to have the secret of immortality.) Gary K. Wolfe notes the gender divide: the women teach school and have children while the men take care of the voyage.[20]

Women in Rock

Grace Slick is one of the most memorable women in rock music history. Some attention to her role as a key member of Jefferson Airplane and Jefferson Starship will remind most readers that the space in which we find a merger of rock music and science fiction has often been a field dominated by men. Women have developed fewer expressions of science fiction rock fantasy. Readers may recall that Patti Smith wrote a song that appeared on her album *Horses*. "Experiment IV" by Kate Bush on her album *The Whole Story* is another notable exception.

It is about a secret military project to create a sound that will kill people. However, many female artists have utilized fantasy or goddess mythology rather than science fiction.

Of course, some vocalists themselves have become mythic or legendary. Slick, Janis Joplin and Patti Smith are regularly cited as being within the rock pantheon. The Wilson sisters of Heart have also achieved similar Rock and Roll Hall of Fame recognition.[21] Perhaps one might say that these women have established their own myths. However, mythology has not been a frequent resource for other female rock artists. Blondie made occasional references to science fiction images. However, they are absent in the music of the Pretenders, Melissa Etheridge, Joan Jett, Pat Benatar, and others. Only occasionally has something mythic or science fiction oriented come through.

Patti Smith, in May 2005, told the British publication *The Guardian* that she turned to art, poetry, and music while feeing a sense of disconnection or feeling alien: "What I wanted to do in rock 'n roll was merge poetry with sonic-scapes."[22] On *Horses*, Patti Smith offers a science fiction reference when she imagines that the son of Wilhelm Reich hallucinates that his father is at the controls of a spaceship. In her androgynous "raggedy glory," said the *Guardian*, her fusion of Rimbaud and rock marked a pivotal movement in the mid to late 1970s that continues to be memorable and influential. That sense of feeling alien and finding mutual connection with others appears to have been crucial to the art that emerged from New York's underground rock scene.

Musician and rock critic Lenny Kaye, guitarist in the Patti Smith Group, has pointed to science fiction's connection with rock. "A lot of the sci-fi fans became hippies," he writes. "You could see these new trends oozing into science fiction; the sense of the counterculture started to break it out of its insular thing." There was a new sense of open possibility and the science fiction imagination connection with rock began moving into the culture. Kaye described himself as "a devoted reader of science fiction," one who collected hundreds of fanzines and read the "double novels" published by Ace. Science fiction was about crossing boundaries. It was a way to imaginatively break out of what he called the "monochrome" fifties and early sixties. As a science fiction fan, he says, "I didn't feel alone in my Otherness."[23] In the

2015 anniversary celebration of the Patti Smith Band's album *Horses* he brought guitar-work again to "Distant Flight," "Birdland," and other songs.

Even with iconic figures like Patti Smith, one might make a case for alienation among women in the rock music industry of the 1960s and 1970s. Since 1990 there has been an increase of attention to women in rock. In "Girls and Subcultures," Jenny Garber comments on a perception of females as consumers of pop music and men of rock music. The claim has been made that females in American culture are closer to consumerism and consequently are more inclined toward pop music than rock.[24] Several female rock acts resist this, although they clearly have entered the pop category. Joan Jett, Pat Benatar, Chrissy Hynde, Melissa Etheridge, who are all commercially popular, have maintained their rock edge.

A question arises: Why do not female rock performers make further use of mythology to assert feminist perspectives or to transform cultural consciousness? Myths may disclose "a level of reality quite beyond any empirical or rational comprehension," observes Mircea Eliade.[25] Christine McVie and Stevie Nicks of Fleetwood Mac brought "Rhiannon" to the pop charts in the 1970s, and Lady Gaga, in her various guises, has appealed to the image of Venus. However, the resources of myth have been tapped more frequently and more notably by male performers than female rock vocalists and musicians.

In Western mythology, there are several models of the goddess. Aphrodite, a goddess of love and sexuality, was honored in the Homeric hymns for her attractiveness, charm, and seductive power. The ancients also called her Ourania, or the sky goddess. For us, she may be both beauty and vanity, the adornment that fuels the cosmetic and fashion industries. She is grace and decoration, Eros and allure. Different images emerge when we look to Athena. She was honored widely and the great city of Athens is named for her. Athena, in *The Odyssey*, is the protector of Odysseus and his son Telemachus. She is a dynamic goddess who stirs them to action. Artemis, known in Roman myth as Diana, was a huntress, a virgin goddess, a figure of purity and moral rectitude who represents nature. Her daughter Daphne was chased by Apollo, who desired her. Yet, the moon is also associated with Artemis (or Diana), the moon goddess. Phoebe, likewise, is a name that is derived from Phoebus, god of the moon, whose name means brilliant and shining. This name is associated with Apollo, as one in whom there is no darkness. Selene (or the Roman Luna) is also a goddess of the moon.

Rock's women have often chosen rebellious and transgressive stances. Some, like Joan Jett, will dress in leather, suggesting urban toughness. Others adopt imagery that underscores that they are experimental, Dionysian, edgy, and bold. They express a dark Eros, an urban savvy, and the soul-power of Hera, Kali, or other poetic figures. They break through bias, chauvinism, and limited viewpoints with their art.

Performers of rock music have also adopted androgynous images, weaving male/female. Consider Patti Smith, wearing a white shirt and dark tie, or David Bowie in jumpsuit and dyed hair. The comparative mythologist Mircea Eliade points to divine androgyny and says that this was often expressed in biological terms, including bisexuality. Such androgyny expresses the coincidence of contraries. He writes: "We must simply note that the divinities of cosmic fertility are, for the most part, either hermaphrodites or male one year and female the next."[26] Eliade lists Attis, Adonis, Dionysius, Cybele the Great Mother, Purusa in the Rig Veda, and Siva Kali. He points out that the gods of Scandinavian mythology, Odin, Loki, Tuisco, and Nerthus retain elements of androgyny.[27] Some traditions hold that the "primeval man" was a hermaphrodite.[28] Perhaps Janis Joplin at her grungiest may suggest this androgyny. But it is the members of Queen, or the New York Dolls, Alice Cooper, or Bowie in whom this androgyny is more apparent.

Gender has been involved in the arguments of some rock critics against "soft," "weak," "light" music. This light pop sound has been identified by some critics as "feminine."[29] These critics favor blues rock with a lack of adornment and critically reject "slick" production, or overproduction. That, on the face of it, may appear a reasonable distinction. However, a problem arises when this becomes gendered into a simple dichotomy that hard rock is male and soft rock and pop is female. Viewed from this perspective Grace Slick seems to be caught within a cultural quandary. One would expect that critics of this disposition would favor the "authentic" blues and folk of the Jefferson Airplane and Hot Tuna to the commercial singles on Jefferson Starship's *Red Octopus* album. The Jefferson Airplane would be viewed as tougher and grittier and Jefferson Starship as lighter pop. Kambrew McLeod observes how rock critics have employed these terms within the discursive space of reviews and asserts that this "tells a story."[30] Such criticism associates tougher and grittier blues rock with masculinity and positions the feminine with the non-progressive, McLeod says.[31] This is the rock critic's sense of the serious, authentic, raw elements of rock versus what the critics consider formulaic fluff.

Some feminist critics of rock have pointed to the masculine posturing of heavy metal bands. Deena Weinstein, among others, rejects the claim that the mythical stance of some heavy metal bands is all that misogynistic. In contrast, Harding and Nett (1984) have called rock blatantly misogynistic. Gottlieb and Wald have viewed rock as deeply masculine. Norma Coates has written of "a constant process of reiteration and the performance of masculinity." Mimi Schippers has argued that "rock culture has relied upon and reproduced quite mainstream ideas about gender and sexuality and in these terms it does not live up to its rebellious counter-cultural image." Schippers points out that songs have often presented stories of the exploitation of women. Coates concludes that some rock songs create an "ultimately fictive masculinity." A stereotypical masculinity is "in play discursively and psychically," Coates says. Deena Weinstein observes that heavy metal celebrates masculinity and Robert Walser notes how it inscribes femininity.[32] Heavy metal masculinity embraces the heroic image, as in the stance of Iron Maiden's Bruce Dickinson and his mythological narratives about heroism and valiant fighting.[33]

However, the goddess figure, the female rock performer—often a vocalist—voices another dimension that is powerful. Grace Slick is one of the forerunners who evoked this power. Grace Slick performed at the 1967 Monterey Pop Festival wearing a flowing white tunic. Psychedelic rock gave attention to visual performance. They sought new world and sang songs with themes of alienation, culture crisis, dissent in relationships, social racial and sexual alienation. They called in "Volunteers," a song written by Balin and Kantner, for a revolution that would be peaceful. Whether Grace Slick, Paul Kantner, and crew were able to create change with their call to revolutionize America is open to question. They became Starship and were successful on the pop music charts with their album *Red Octopus*, which featured the hit single "Miracles." Perhaps, in the end, it can at least be said that they bravely used science fiction and myth to gesture toward the miraculous.

FOUR

The Electric Light Orchestra

Science Fiction with Strings Attached

With their album *Time* (1981), ELO—the Electric Light Orchestra—connected science fiction and the pop song. They joined the gallery of radio singles like Zager and Evans' "In the Year 2525," David Bowie's "Space Oddity," and Elton John's "Rocket Man." ELO emerged from the British band the Move in the early 1970s when Roy Wood imagined a rock orchestra in which rock guitars and drums met with violins and cellos. On July 12, 1970, Wood added multiple cellos to a track.[1] He was joined by drummer Bev Bevan, guitarist and songwriter Jeff Lynne, Bill Hunt on horns and keyboards, and violinist Steve Woolam. Jeff Lynne, from the Idle Race, would become the leader of ELO as Wood moved on to solo work and recording with his band Wizzard.

The science fiction themed *Time* is among the most popular of ELO's albums. It was a pivotal recording in the career of a band that would have twenty top 40 singles and sell more than 50 million records globally.[2] ELO emerged from Birmingham, where blues and rock were popular. From the industrial city came the Move, the Moody Blues, the Spencer Davis Group, Traffic, Judas Priest, Black Sabbath, and members of Led Zeppelin. Birmingham has been described as "the cradle of all things heavy" and has been called a birthplace for heavy metal. The ELO concept was to orchestrate a pop/rock sound with string instruments. In contrast with some of the Birmingham bands, ELO would be a pop singles oriented band. The rock and roll based Mersey beat was important to ELO and their tuneful creations launched them increasingly in a pop direction. The imagination of Roy Wood pushed them toward myth and the fantastic. Jeff Lynne would move ELO toward the science fiction concepts of *Time.*

While developing their first album, ELO played their first gig at the Greyhound Pub in Croydon, Surrey. Their first single "10538 Overture" may sound like a date in the future but it concerned the number of an escaped prisoner. During the recording of their second album Wood left ELO and formed Wizzard. Lynne and Bevan reconstituted the band with Mike Edwards (cello), Wilfred Gibson (violin) and Richard Tandy (bass and synthesizer). The "Electric Light" in the group's name appeared as a light bulb on early album covers. "Electric" meant electric orchestral instruments, plugged in. A "light" orchestra was one with only some instruments: in this case, mostly cellos and violins. Rich harmony vocals and large orchestration proved to be an effective combination. The debut record was initially released in America as *No Answer.* There would be eleven studio albums between 1971 and 1986. Lynne, Bevan, and Tandy remained at the core of the band, which brought in an array of string players and other musicians.

The second ELO album was to be "The Lost Planet": a clear reference to science fiction ideas. It was released as ELO II (1973) with cover art by the Japanese artist Shusei Nagaoka that featured a spaceship. ELO had begun to engage in science fiction reflections on space and the cosmos, time, and robotics. The record featured the single "Roll Over Beethoven" and the science fiction cuts "From the Sun to the World" (Boogie #1) and "Kuiama." The album was followed by *On the Third Day* (1973) and *Eldorado: A Symphony* (1974). Jeff Lynne became the creative center and director of *Eldorado,* which included the single "Can't Get It Out of My Head." The songs on the album create the image of a dreamer who gets lost in a dreamworld that becomes his life, in a way that is similar to the fictional character Walter Mitty.

Face the Music (1975) brought the hit singles "Evil Woman" and "Strange Magic." During the course of the third album, ELO again made personnel changes. The band grew in popularity as they received wide airplay and began to place single after single on the charts. There were colored lasers for the concerts that supported ELO's next album, *A New World Record* (1976), which featured the single "Telephone Line," and "Do Ya," a remake of the Move song with its repeating D-A-G power chord pattern. ELO remained hot on the charts with "Living Thing." *Out of the Blue* (1977), which followed, is a double-album with a cover by Shusei Nagaoka that bears the ELO logo of a jukebox which has become a spaceship. ELO made use of this spaceship design for their stage set for concerts. Curiously, there were no science fiction themed songs on the album.

Time

With *Time*, ELO clearly entered the realm of the science fiction concept album. Set in the beginning of the twenty-first century, the lyrics are framed by a story about a man who falls in love with a robot. This provided an opportunity to note some references by science fiction writers and scientists to robotics. ELO added a heavy use of synthesizers to its layered choral vocals for this album. In 1980, immediately before beginning work on *Time*, Jeff Lynne had been asked to compose music for the film *Xanadu*. Bev Bevan had recently produced his memoirs, *The ELO Story* (1980). The science fiction concept album emerged alongside the idea of bringing a further progressive rock edge to ELO's sound. Synthesizers, like the DX7, were coming into use at this time and they contributed an electronic futuristic sense to the album.

ELO also largely replaced the big string section that they were noted for. Some strings were added to the mix in the studio. However, this was a progressive rock album with Louis Clark's synthesizers and vocals, Dave Morgan's guitar, synthesizer, and vocals, and Mik Kaminski playing on his blue violin. The album brought songs with this new approach: "Hold on Tight," Twilight," "The Way Life's Meant to Be," "Here is the News," and "Ticket to the Moon." Fred the Robot voiced the Prologue and Epilogue on the band's tour.

The changes on this album were striking. Along with the narrative concept of a man's startling passion for a robot there was the obvious shift in the band's sound: a stronger emphasis upon synthesizers, guitars, and choral vocals. We hear songs like "Golden Age," which uses science fiction as a basis for inquiry into the future and to create a musical suite. The album begins with synthesizer chords in "Prologue."

A robotic distorted voice breaks through the music and points to fantasy and a message from another time. The up-tempo pulse is accompanied by lyrics that provide suggestions of dawn visions and twilight dreams. ELO's characteristic vocals are featured prominently but the ELO sound has clearly become dominated by synthesizers rather than by a symphonic string section. This is a keyboard saturated overture with a driving beat. ("Twilight" would later be used for a Daicon IV science fiction convention in 1983.) "Rain Is Falling" follows, with its opening passages washed with the sounds of rain. The sound effect of thunder is met by the lead vocal and high chorus vocals. The drums maintain a regular 4/4 time and violins pulse. The vocalist/narrator says that despite his intentions, goals, and dreams, he stays in the same place. The vocal comes to us underneath the higher tones of the keyboards.

On "Yours Truly, 2095" a distant boys-choir sound is covered by music that races along and the muffled, robotic voice we heard in "Prologue" returns. The theme of time is stated by the lead vocalist who declares that he has sent a message to some other place in the future, to another time. Then he begins to critique a female figure that is described as cold and mechanical. She is similar to you, he tells the listener, but she's an IBM wearing a jumpsuit. She is cool like the most up-to-date technology but watch out for that stone-cold heart. The music romps along in double-time with keyboards and chorus vocals singing above the melody line.

"Here Is the News" gives us a lead vocal that in answered by a studio-compressed vocal and spoken news reports that are surrounded by layered chorale vocals. The up-tempo energy is propelled by the drums and the keyboards simulate the higher melodic and harmonic figures of strings.

"Ticket to the Moon" is a ballad introduced by piano and a solo voice. The vocalist-narrator tells listeners that he will be traveling to the moon and has to get ready for the journey. He would prefer to stay home, looking into his lover's eyes and at the sunrise he sees there. This song moves into a strong vocal chorus in which there is melodic movement. At times the music suggests a sense of drifting in space, a sense of floating that is supported by the orchestration. "Ticket to the Moon," with its often repeated title, may be likened to a small orchestral suite.

"The Way Life Is Meant to Be" begins cinematically. Guitars support the vocal narrative in which the speaker, landing in a strange territory, recognizes that he is a stranger. The band plays music that is fairly predictable, utilizing pop chord patterns reminiscent of Spanish/Latino music. This proceeds toward "Another Heart Breaks," an instrumental that begins with Bev Bevan's drums. The bass guitar joins in and a keyboard pattern begins over this. The album's hit song "Hold On Tight," a top ten single, offers sounds out of late 1950s rock and roll with a vocal that is suggestive of Roy Orbison. (Jeff Lynne would later work with Orbison in the first incarnation of The Traveling Wilburys.) The lyric adds some French into the mix. The tune is catchy and the song is rhythmically infectious. It probably would serve for a good workout in an aerobics class. With its rockabilly atmosphere and positive message it is a simpler composition than many of the others on this album.

"From the End of the World" is a song that is based in synthesizers and it ramps up with a running bass line. The vocal is filled with reverb and joins straight ahead drumming, synthesizer, and ELO's characteristic high vocals. On "Twenty-First Century Man" a solo vocal tells the story of what it is like to live in the twenty-first century. What will it be like to be a man holding a suitcase and flying off to work? The experience is one of being a hero one day and completely down the next. Perhaps this is the life of a rock star who is acclaimed one day and a critical cast-off the next. There is a luxurious slide guitar break in the bridge of this song. One might imagine John Lennon singing the vocal with the Beatles, post–*Abbey Road*. ELO flies into the future with a suggestion of that musical past and what it might have become. These songs were familiar to their audience as ELO took them on the road.

The ELO entourage traveled a great deal on their tour and they experienced the ups and downs of their twenty-first century man within a music industry filled with changes. Their album spoke of humanity's interaction with robots and of a ticket to the moon. Yet, *Time* flew further in its implications. Music itself is within time. Its melodies, harmonic and rhythmic patterns flow as an art of time.

In 1905, Albert Einstein gave us a new concept of time. His landmark discovery appeared in his essay "On the Electrodynamics of Moving Bodies." Einstein held that if the speed of light is consistent for each of two observers in motion at a constant velocity space and time are not separate. Einstein later developed the General Theory of Relativity and published three consequential papers in November 1915.[3] The mystery of time or time travel to the stars that opened before humanity in the twentieth century lay behind ELO's speculations about twenty-first century man. The song recognizes that we are limited in relation to the speed of light and that the stars are light years away. A person might go to the moon but could one ever travel to the stars? One would have to travel near the speed of light to reach those stars within the span of a lifetime. Might there be another way?

Our ideas about time have changed over the centuries. Isaac Newton once called time absolute and universal and for him time was everywhere the same in the universe. ELO's twentieth-century man knows otherwise. Einstein challenged the Newtonian perspective and revolutionized our sense of time. The rate of time's passage is different for two observers who are in motion. Those two observers do not feel time passing at the same rate. Einstein showed that the passage of time depended upon the strength of the gravitational field in which the observer stood. In Pink Floyd's "Time" on *Dark Side of the Moon* (1973) a variety of clocks sound simultaneously. In ELO's *Time*, songs explore the arrow of time and romance in up-tempo pop.

Time was ELO's last album to go platinum. Their albums *Eldorado* and *Discovery* did well commercially but ELO could only have limited staying power into the 1980s. Jeff Lynne sought to follow this effort with a double album. Lynne was stretching out with his music production abilities. The band continued to be popular and its fans probably would have responded well to the double album. CBS, the band's record company, said no. It would be too expensive, they concluded. Instead, the next project became *Secret Messages* (1983). The band had not yet let go of its science fiction motifs. "Out of the Blue" turned a logo into a spaceship flying saucer. In many respects, ELO began to dissolve thereafter.[4]

Roy Wood's Wizzard

Roy Wood, meanwhile, played a role in glam, psychedelic, and progressive rock. His solo albums included *Boulders* (1973) and

Mustard (1975), with vocal appearances from Annie Haslam and Phil Everly. The band's name suggests musical magic. They performed their first concert at Wembley stadium on August 5, 1972, and then went on to play at the Reading Festival.

As ELO became the consummate pop singles band, Roy Wood took a different direction. Wood costumed his glam rock act. *Wizzard's Brew* (1973) was a jazz inflected recording. Wizzard's next recording, *Introducing Eddie and the Falcons* (1974), was styled more commercially. Wood also released his solo albums *Boulders* (1973) and *Mustard* (1975). Wizzard dissolved in 1975. Warner Bros., their record company, found the recording *Main Street* was not commercial enough and the record languished. In 2000, *Main Street* finally was released. Wizzard produced several non-album singles: "Ball Park Incident," "See My Baby Jive," "Angel Fingers," "This Is the Story of My Love," and "I Wish It Could Be Christmas Everyday." Wood had clearly taken a progressive and less commercial direction with his music, away from the pop orientation of his former band mates with ELO.

ELO's sheer pop music popularity may have caused some grumbles from people who rejected formulaic pop or shallow escapism. Yet, they were accomplished musicians with a strong sense of vocal harmony. They emphasized studio production and arrangements that some people found overblown. Rock musicians may dissociate themselves from pop music, regarding what they do as a separate art. At an MTV activity Axl Rose of Guns N' Roses, in 1992, declared: "This has nothing to do with Michael Jackson."[5] He might have added that his band's music had nothing to do with bands like ELO either.

A Note on Recording

ELO kept up with changes in recording techniques and varied their sound as they moved into the 1980s. Most recordings shifted from analog to digital during the 1980s. ELO, as a pop singles band, was by then ripe for re-mastering into greatest hits compilations. Digital recording and computers began to change the industry. The digital computer processes numerical information. A Pro Tools system in a recording studio casts a dance of colored bands of light that may be interesting to watch but a great deal is going on that does not meet the eye. The computer handles symbolic information by using binary digits known as bits. The data processing elements are in the integrated circuits that make up the microprocessor. The computer has data storage and or memory. A compact disc will store millions of sixteen bit "words" on a recording. Several progressive rock producers and performing musicians, from Alan Parsons to Todd Rundgren to Geddy Lee, have become extremely savvy about how to get sounds from technology in the concert setting as well as in the studio.

Musical acoustics remains an ongoing issue for rock musicians who are plugged in as well as those who are "unplugged." This is an area of acoustics that deals with musical instruments and how sound reaches the listener. Of course this is particularly important for a band's use of acoustic guitars, or ELO's cellos, or Ian Anderson's flute playing with Jethro Tull. It is also quite important for drums and percussion and for vocals. In the case of ELO's cellists, the musician puts energy into the vibration of the strings. The flow of energy exists within a vibrating system. In the case of Ian Anderson, he plays the flute with breath and the input valve is flow controlled. Musical sound has volume, pitch, timbre, and the duration of the notes that are played. Pitch is the tone low to high that we usually associate with a musical scale. Timbre is associated with tone color. It is a quality that depends upon the overall pattern of sound, waveform, and sound pressure. The instrument and the room sound will affect what is heard. The piano is a string instrument that produces music through vibration. It is also a percussion instrument because keys are struck by the player. When the acoustic piano is played the "room sound" in which the instrument is played is significant.[6]

Seeking a spacious, contemporary sound, ELO transitioned from acoustic instruments to synthesizers. Electronic instruments produce tones that are available for amplification. The electric guitar will sound thin and tinny unless it is plugged in. Then, with the aid of a variety of effects, it can become a monster. In the 1960s organ sounds were joined by Moog keyboards. Synthesizers developed based on frequency modulation using oscillators. With the 1980s came digital sampling, which involves playing back recorded material and manipulated sound. ELO was one of many groups that showed that synthesizers can achieve a wide variety of sounds. However, it is often difficult to reproduce the sounds of many of the acoustic instruments ELO played with great fidelity. Some programs reflect the sounds of acoustic piano remarkably well. However, solo woodwinds and bowed string instruments are difficult to imitate precisely, as this requires a lot of memory in the system.

Jeff Lynne, Alone in the Universe

Jeff Lynne remained a productive pop music innovator throughout the 1980s and 1990s. He took on musical collaborations, producing George Harrison's *Cloud Nine* and other recordings. He produced the Traveling Wilburys, a playful collective, in which he made music with Bob Dylan, George Harrison, Roy Orbison, and Tom Petty.[7] ELO's *Flashback* (2000) reunited the band for a boxed set retrospective of three CDs and a tour. ELO's version of "Xanadu" reached number one in England. With an album titled *Zoom,* Jeff Lynne returned to the ELO melodic pop form with a record that let go of much of the band's former penchant for orchestration. Ringo Starr makes a guest appearance on two cuts on the album ("Moment in Paradise" and "Easy Money"). A new cast of musicians joined Lynne and longtime associate Richard Tandy (keyboards): Rosie Kela (vocals), Marc Mann (guitar and keyboards), Matt Bisonette and George Bisonette as the rhythm section, and Peggy Baldwin and Nancy Ross on cellos.

Jeff Lynne used the spaceship logo for his 2016 tour, which followed the album *Alone in the Universe.* Lynne developed the record with Tandy and it was released November 13, 2015, the first ELO album in more than a decade. The single "When I Was a Boy" has an almost McCartney Beatlesesque sound. Clearly, Jeff Lynne's revisiting ELO with a new sound continues a personal statement and suggests a sense of something cosmic and universal at the center of musical creativity.

FIVE

David Bowie

From Major Tom to Ziggy Stardust

David Bowie will always be associated with science fiction. Soon after signing his contract with RCA Records, David Bowie became Ziggy Stardust. This was a transformation of his image that was intended to be outrageous and compelling while consistent with his artistic vision. Each of Bowie's reconfigurations drew him into the spotlight of rock criticism and contributed to making him one of the most studied of rock performers.

Bowie frequently transformed himself into a mythical creature. He remade his sound and his image over several times. In November 1971 RCA Records released *Hunky Dory*, with the single "Changes." It was an album that some executives at RCA did not especially like. In January 1972 some fourteen concert dates were set for February and March. Bowie's management, led by Dennis Katz, sought to develop publicity for Bowie in the United States. During this time, Bowie's band, led by guitarist Mick Ronson, was becoming the Spiders from Mars. Their act was artifice, cosmetics, and costuming; it was intended to be theatrical. The band was outfitted in gold suits and Bowie developed his androgynous character of Ziggy: an otherworldly hermaphrodite, a gender bending guitar playing creature somewhere in between male and female. His team thought about merchandising Ziggy dolls and boots. He drew upon his respect for Lou Reed and the Velvet Underground as the band played "White Light, White Heat" and "Waiting for the Man" alongside Bowie singles like "Suffragette City." He took cues from Marc Bolan, Iggy Pop, the New York Dolls, and Alice

Cooper's shows. He created an act, a science fiction persona that his art could speak through. *Melody Maker* called David Bowie and his band "superb parodists." Bowie told a *Rolling Stone* magazine photojournalist that his character of Ziggy was a cartoon. Yet, there was uniqueness and drama to this otherworldly character, this comic book creation. There was also in Ziggy Stardust an expression of Bowie's creativity and the malleability of the artist.

Space Oddity, in 1969, suggested Bowie's interest in other worlds and science fiction. The release of the record coincided with the Apollo mission's launch to the moon in 1969. Re-released in 1972, the single about Major Tom became a popular hit and a signature song for Bowie. The listener is immediately drawn into reflection upon humanity's ventures to outer space. In March 1972, "Starman" was the first single from *The Rise and Fall of Ziggy Stardust and the Spiders from Mars*. "Five Years" begins the recording ominously with a note of world crisis, the news that the world has only five years of existence left. In "Starman" the narrator is a child who sees a UFO. He tells his friends and he contacts the Starman. At the center of the record are the songs "Ziggy Stardust," "Suffragette City," and the record's closer "Rock 'n' Roll Suicide." Underlying this recording is a critique of art and the recording industry, of creation, construction, and manufacture. Bowie appears to reflect upon his own constructed image and upon the ways in which the industry and society creates pop stars. We hear about Ziggy, who played guitar and who seems to be a figure caught up in what some commentators on Bowie have called a "self-destruct mechanism."[1]

Bowie experimented with constructions of identity and character throughout his career. Bowie's characters represent the "periodic ecstatic self-annihilation" and rebirth of a Dionysian figure, a Phoenix that renews himself, critics have pointed out. "His other great inspiration is mythology," stated Gordon Coxkill, an early interviewer. The interviewer said that Bowie had a need to believe in legends like Atlantis and that "he has crafted a myth of the future," of a superior race. He placed Bowie within rock's history of "shock and outrage."[2]

"It's a brave new world and either we join it or we become relics," Bowie told another music critic.[3] He spoke of his music and art as participating in "a wave of the future." He acknowledged his bisexuality in a *Melody Maker* interview and this became news. His sexual orientation had been part of the life of David Jones before he became David Bowie, or the character of Ziggy Stardust. Bowie rejected any labels regarding the sexual orientation of individuals. Meanwhile, his management capitalized on the press swirling around him and announced a tour of England for summer 1972. That would be followed by an eight city tour in the United States. Capping this tour was a successful sold-out concert in Cleveland in the 3,500 seat Cleveland Music Hall. Ziggy Stardust was now a headliner, a rock "star." David Bowie had arrived.

A great deal has been written on Bowie. The writer of *Hallo Spaceboy*, Dave Thompson, calls Bowie "the biggest thing in the 1970s consciousness."[4] Frith and Horne see Bowie as creating "a blank canvas on which consumers write their dreams." Bowie is "a modern heroic figure."[5] In his introduction to *The Man Who Sold the World: David Bowie in the 1970s*, Peter Doggett calls him "popular culture's most reliable guide to the fever of the seventies."[6] Some analysis of that "fever" might be called for. One commentator, Christopher Lasch, called the decade "the age of narcissisism."[7] Doggett recognizes Lasch's book and Tom Wolfe's phrase "the me-decade." He calls the sixties an "era of progress" and no doubt strides were made in civil rights, women's rights, and environmental awareness but was the 1960s a period of more "progress" than the 1970s, which the author describes as a time of "dread and misgiving," of "hedonism and power failures."[8] Doggett proceeds to make a fine case for seeing Bowie as an important voice in the 1970s (and in the revivals of his career beyond this). Other critics have frequently seen reflections of contemporary culture throughout his work. However, to call Bowie the "the biggest thing in the 1970s consciousness," as Thompson does, or the "most reliable guide" to the 1970s in all of popular culture, as Doggett asserts, are claims that have to be qualified.

Bowie brought together rock with pantomime and with science fiction. The ongoing science fiction motif is a constant in Bowie's career, appearing in Major Tom, Ziggy Stadust, *The Man Who Fell to Earth*, and Earthling. Bowie was interested in the possibility of extraterrestrial life and UFOs. He liked science fiction films like Stanley Kubrick's *2001* and *A Clockwork Orange* and Ridley Scott's *Blade Runner*. In 2002 Bowie also mentioned a surrealist influence from the artists Man Ray, Dali, Bunuel, and the film *Un Chien Andalou*. Bowie was visually oriented and he once called his some of his songs "paintings in words." He was consciously an actor and performer. To Gordon Coxkill, Bowie spoke of his need for an audience's response and his desire to entertain. In that interview he recalled meeting Marc Bolan and having recently been on tour with Humble Pie as their opener. He spoke of the value of clubs and cabarets.

David Bowie has fascinated audiences and critics because he has continually revised and recast himself. He has been called "a manipulator of pop tastes."[9] but he also was always an artist engaged in self-discovery. David Buckley refers to Bowie as an imaginative autodidact: that is, a person who is self-educated. Early on his book on Bowie he refers to the musician's "melismatic, creaky, almost asthmatic saxophone playing."[10] He quotes Paul Buckmaster saying that Bowie was moved by "the whole sci-fi vibe which had invaded popular culture."[11] Buckmaster's talks with Bowie concerned aliens and UFOs, figures recalled from comics and science fiction literature. This was "a sort of pop science fiction mysticism mixed with a bit of metaphysics and spiritualism." Meanwhile, Bowie's friend Lesley Duncan talked about UFOs.[12]

As a child, David Jones became fascinated with science fiction. He lived at 40 Stansfield Road in Brixton. His family then moved to Bromley, the town in which H.G. Wells was born. The BBC science fiction series *Quatermass Experiment* had an impact on Bowie. Paul Trynka observes that David Jones's absorption in the series "sparked a lifelong fascination with science fiction."[13] Marc Spitz says that the *Quatermass Experiment* probably "introduced David Jones to the concept of outer space" and encouraged Bowie to imagine space exploration. He argues that this image offered him a sense of potential to break out of the repression he experienced in his environment.[14] Wendy Leigh points out that his parents thought that the *Quatermass II* series was "too adult" for him.[15] Early on in his music making, his band The Lower Third, formed at Margate near Kent in 1964–65, did the "Mars" theme from Gustav Holst's *The Planets*, which he had heard on *Quatermass*.

Bowie's science fiction references in his songs appear to relate to metaphysical questioning and reflections on identity and rock music stardom. Bowie told the *Los Angeles Times* that he used "science fiction patterns because I was trying to put forward concepts, ideas, and theories but this album hasn't anything to do with that. It's just emotional drive."[16] He was talking about a future recording, *Diamond Dogs*, on which appears "1984." He told the interviewer that "Space Oddity" was quite personal. In his discussion of the song, Michael Mooradian Lupro observes that Bowie "inhabits discrete and contradictory spaces" that we can all travel to "the brightest star in space and rock." He developed "alternative spaces." While "playing with stardom," Bowie was using space "as a place to locate difference." Lupro notes that "space technology themes" are "a consistent source of empowerment through which marginalized voices are given a safe forum for the exploration of new modes of identity."[17]

Bowie's value lies in drawing our attention to "transformations of the self," observes Richard Fitch. His art is engaged in "a postmodern politics of fluid identity."[18] Bowie's personas invite postmodern reflection on just what it means to be human. Ellen Willis wrote: "A lot of nonsense has been written about Bowie—ubiquitous comparisons to Alice Cooper can only be willful incomprehension." She concluded that Bowie was glitter and not at all troubling. "There is nothing provocative, perverse, or revolting about Bowie. He is all glitter, no grease." The bi-sexuality is "not that big a deal," Willis added. Androgyny has always been present in British rock. Bowie is a "polished pop surface," not decadence. Underneath the Day-Glo he is a folkie who likes Jacques Brel. His dyed red hair, makeup, dresses are theatrical.[19]

The science fiction framework chosen for the figure of Ziggy Stardust, with his band the Spiders from Mars, welcomes us to think about aliens and alienation and about the reinventions of the human that run through science fiction stories. Bowie calls us to give thought to media constructions of celebrity and to the disintegration and eclipse of some of these figures. He carried this mythical mode from the height of his acclaim with records like *Aladdin Sane* and *Young Americans* in the 1970s into other phases of his career. This mythical mode was present in the revival of his work in the 1990s and the farewell that he created for his final album when he knew that his death was imminent in 2016.

In Bowie's last recording he pours himself out with a final affirmation of a life dedicated to creativity. The poet Rainer Maria Rilke, in his *Sonnets to Orpheus* (1966), encouraged the artist to never "shut himself in abiding" but "to pour himself out as a spring" and to "will transformation," like a flame that will change and gain power. Bowie again faced the changes, as he declared in one of his early singles. In his final recording he embraced dying and transformed this into art. This was what the poet Keats once called negative capability. It was an affirmation, giving himself to the creative force. Bowie's farewell was, in every sense, the gift and last testament of a multi-faceted artist.

A Space Oddity

With "Space Oddity" (1969) Bowie was signed to Mercury Records and his song about Major Tom was connected with the July 1969 Apollo space mission to the moon.[20] The song emerged after Bowie's father's death from pneumonia, August 5, 1969. Zager and Evans' hit single "In the Year 2525" was on the charts a few weeks earlier than "Space Oddity." Bowie's song was re-released in 1972 and became a hit single and one of his signature songs.

"Space Oddity" has drawn considerable commentary. Critics have seen Stanley Kubrick's adaptation of Arthur C. Clarke's *2001* as one source for Bowie narrative. Carmen Paglia has viewed "Space Oddity" as "a requiem" for the age of hippies and "flower power." Major Tom was Bowie's "psychedelic astronaut." Wendy Leigh observes that the song along with "Life on Mars" and "Starman" "insured that he would be forever associated with the planets, space, the moon, and the stars." In her view, Bowie "punctured the global admiration for the Apollo mission to the moon." This seems like a rather large claim. Van Cagle sees Major Tom as a Luddite who is suicidal. Phil Auslander views "Space Oddity" as a technophobic response of the counterculture. "Tom is helpless to address the world's ills," he says. Michael Mooradian Lupro, in contrast to this, sees Major Tom as "an active participant in altering the conditions of his labor." He cannot be controlled. Lupro argues that Major Tom is resistant to the control of Ground Control; he is transgressive and breaks free. Yet, perhaps Major Tom's attention is drawn away from his mission simply by his wonder at the stars.

Linking Bowie's song to Kubrick's film *2001: A Space Odyssey*,

Marc Spitz conjectures that the song was inspired by a scene of the astronaut responding from space to his daughter on her birthday. Of course, Bowie's song was likely inspired by many more things than this particular scene. Spitz attempts to psychoanalyze Bowie, suggesting that scenes like this suggest a family connection that appealed to David Bowie who lacked security and attention in his home in childhood.[21] However we may read this, it does appear that Major Tom finds liberty in drifting away, even if one sees in this a doomed floating forever in space.

The Spaceman Enters

Bowie used the rock star as outsider and extra-terrestrial theme in *The Rise and Fall of Ziggy Stardust and the Spiders from Mars.* The androgynous figure raises questions about the construction of gender. Bowie's acoustic guitar playing is heard throughout the album: a twist on the notion of folk music authenticity. Bowie clearly can rock. "Rock 'n' Roll Suicide" brings the album to a strong conclusion.

So, who was Bowie now? In October 1972, Ellen Willis wrote: "In England Bowie may already be "a red star" but in the American context he looks more like an aesthete using stardom as a metaphor." Yet, she notes that she is "not entirely happy" with this perspective. She had quickly become a fan. At Bowie's Carnegie Hall debut she stood on her seat.[22] *Hunky Dory* (1971) was a favorite of hers. The song "Life on Mars" was on that album but the science fiction motif was not conspicuous. She expected "a soft, vague sensibility" from the cover photograph. "Instead, Bowie turned out to be an intelligent, disciplined, wry Lou Reed freak," she wrote.[23]

Then along came the Ziggy persona to disrupt that view further: "But the idea of a pop star from outer space (read pop star as explorer, prophet, poet of technology, exotic on the outside but merely human on the inside and so on) just doesn't make it—except maybe as a spoof."[24] Peter Doggett notes that Bowie beamed "the smile of the spaceman" in a BBC television performance, indicating that he was "not taking any of this seriously."[25] Willis, however, notes that Ziggy Stardust "seems to take it seriously." She points out "Bowie's flash and control. On the train, Owen has no money and he is given a loan by the Anarchist. (We hear of him in the fourth cut on the record, "The Anarchist.") The Anarchist faces off against the Watchmaker, who asserts that "the universe has a plan: all is for the best." Owen gets caught up in a plot that might remind one of the anarchism in Joseph Conrad's *The Secret Agent.* The anarchist implicates him in a bombing and Owen is on the run.

Clockwork Angels sold well. It received Canada's Juno Award for best album of the year in 2013 and led Peart to explore writing "2113," as a sequel to *2112.* He imagined a new recording: *Clockwork Lives.* Peart also wrote another memoir: *Far and Near: On Days Like These* (October 2014.)

Rush's entry into the Rock and Roll Hall of Fame was a peak of public recognition for the band's a long career of innovative musicianship and fiercely independent thinking. Science fiction has figured significantly in their journey. They have brought science fiction concepts, images, and social critique into connection with their idiosyncratic style of progressive rock. The imagination of Rush has embraced technology fervently, while warning against excesses of scientism or political control and asserting the dignity and rights of individuals to be as unique as they choose to be.

NINE

The Alan Parsons Project
Robots and Telepathy

Mystery, science fiction, and drama converge in the smooth, lush sound produced by the musicianship and technological skills of the Alan Parsons Project. Ten studio albums and a string of hit singles that might be classified as easy listening rock came from this musical collective in which the studio recording talents of Alan Parsons were matched with the songwriting skills of Eric Woolfson. They brought together a cast of vocalists and musicians to create some of the most memorable pop music of the 1970s and early 1980s.

The Alan Parsons Project, at first, was never quite what we would call a rock band. It consisted of two very talented studio-minded musicians, Parsons and Eric Woolfson, who created many gold and platinum albums and utilized guest vocalists. Woolfson was the songwriter, coming up with a string of easy listening light rock hits and several science fiction concept albums. Parsons was a renowned recording engineer and producer, who was an assistant recording engineer for the Beatles' *Abbey Road* and *Let It Be* and the recording engineer for Pink Floyd's *The Dark Side of the Moon* (1974). He had produced albums for Ambrosia, Al Stewart, and Pilot. Woolfson and Parsons displayed a technological mastery of the recording studio and a penchant for exploring the mysterious and a variety of science fiction themes. They offered speculations on robots, time, and electronic and satellite surveillance. The Alan Parsons Project scored several radio friendly singles on their first albums and broke out commercially with the vocal by Woolfson on his song "Eye in the Sky" in 1982. The song remotely reflects Philip K. Dick's novel *Eye in the Sky* (1957). Its haunting melody and arrangement captures a creepy surveillance theme in an atmosphere enhanced by smooth vocal harmonies.

Parsons and Woolfson met in the early 1970s, when Woolfson pursued music management to supplement his career as a songwriter. Parsons, a talented music arranger and studio engineer, became one of his first clients. Alan Parsons began his career by working at the EMI tape duplicating facility at Abbey Road. There he met The Beatles and worked as an assistant, studying their remarkable work on *Sgt. Pepper* and the Beatles' subsequent recordings. His work continued with Paul McCartney on *Wild Life* and *Red Rose Speedway*, and, most significantly, he recorded Pink Floyd's *Dark Side of the Moon*. Parsons also recorded three albums with Pilot, with Ian Bairnson on guitar, Stuart Tosk on drums, Billy Lyell on keyboards, and David Paton's vocals. He developed three albums with Al Stewart, including the singles "Time Passages" and "The Year of the Cat," jazzing up Stewart's folk-based music and adding the familiar saxophone part. With the Hollies, Parsons produced five albums, including their hit recording of the Neil Diamond song "He Ain't Heavy, He's My Brother" and their recording of "The Air That I Breathe." He mixed Ambrosia's first album and was involved with their recording *Somewhere I've Never Traveled*. Parsons declined to work on Pink Floyd's *Wish You Were Here* because he was beginning work with Woolfson on the Alan Parsons Project.

Woolfson was born in Glasgow on March 18, 1945. He was fascinated with science fiction and mystery stories. His uncle played piano and that encouraged Woolfson to take piano lessons as a child. He abandoned formal lessons and was mostly self-taught. He eventually became a session pianist and spent time on London's Denmark Street, a music center. He met Jimmy Page and John Paul Jones in the years before their formation of Led Zeppelin. He then met Andrew Oldham, the manager of the Rolling Stones, who was impressed by his songs and gave him a publishing deal with Immediate Records. Woolfson's songs were recorded by Marianne Faithful, Frank Field and others. His early recordings included a Chris Farlowe B-side on "Out of Time." Woolfson met Tim Rice and Andrew Lloyd Webber at Southern Music, as they were turning their attention to the musical theater. Attempting to make a living in the music business, Woolfson he became an independent record producer and he tried out artist management. Carl Douglas, whose "Kung Fu Fighting" reached the pop charts in 1974, became one of his clients. However, more important for his future was his new association with producer Parsons. The Alan Parsons Project emerged from that partnership. Woolfson was deeply involved with all of the group's hits. In the late 1980s Woolfson focused on musical theater.

The science fiction concepts of Woolfson were often expressed on record with spacious effects and synthesizers. They were enriched by with the masterful studio technology of Alan Parsons. In 1976, Woolfson had recently finished adapting four of Edgar Alan Poe's stories and two of Poe's poems. Parsons produced and engineered the *Tales of Mystery and Imagination* (1976) album, bringing lush instrumentation to an album based in themes that were largely conceived of by Woolfson.[1]

The Image of the Robot

For their second album, the Alan Parsons Project turned to Isaac Asimov's novel *I, Robot* for inspiration and explored the potential of artificial intelligence. *I Robot* (1977) is often considered the masterpiece of the Alan Parsons Project and it has been re-released in an extended version titled *Legacy*. Eric Woolfson spoke with Isaac Asimov as he prepared the songs for this recording. Asimov approved of the project. The rights for *I, Robot* had been given to a television movie company. At the same time that Eric Woolfson arrived at the idea for a concept album, Harlan Ellison was adapting the nine stories for a screenplay. *I Robot* used the title of Isaac Asimov's book but dropped the comma in that title. In Asimov's novel, Dr. Susan Calvin tells stories to the narrator, who is a reporter in the twenty-first century. Woolfson seized upon this scheme for a narrative pattern for his songs. The album offers a narrative about robots and human wills in conflict with each other.

According to the album liner notes, Woolfson structured the album thematically around the idea of "The story of the rise of the machine and the decline of man."[2] This occurred when the human "tried to re-create the robot in his own image." The record ends with "Genesis, Chapter 1, Verse 32," a speculation that takes us beyond the text, since the written biblical document of *Genesis* has 31 verses. Woolfson created an eclectic weave of songs and instrumentals and brought together a collective of musicians from the bands Pilot and Ambrosia, whose recordings Parsons produced at the time. The musicians included David Paton on acoustic guitar and bass, Stuart Tosh on drums, Ian Bairnson on guitars, B.J. Cole on steel pedal, John Leach on cymbalon and kantele, and Duncan Mackay, who added keyboards.

On the album cover, the Alan Parsons Project is featured in a hazy photo of band members crossing the escalator tubes of circular Terminal 1 at Charles De Gaulle Airport near Paris. Over this is superimposed a painting of a robot. The singles "I Wouldn't Want to Be Like You" and "Don't Let It Show" became hits that are still often played on classic rock and album oriented rock (AOR) stations. "Day After Day (The Show Must Go On)" also reached the charts. The song "Breakdown" has had a long life in radio play on AOR stations. The album's opening cut is the instrumental "I, Robot." The vocal on "I Wouldn't Want to Be Like You," which follows, is by Lenny Zakatek, a vocalist often featured among the Parsons revolving cast of singers. The musical journey continues with Peter Staker's vocal, along with Jaki Wittren singing on "Some Other Time." "Breakdown" features the singing of Allan Clarke, a key member of the Hollies. Dave Townsend's vocal on "Don't Let It Show" ends the first side of the LP. When listeners turned the vinyl record over they heard Steve Harley singing on "The Voice." "Nucleus," with its obvious science derived title, provided an instrumental break before "Day After Day" with Jack Harris' vocal. The instrumental of "Total Eclipse" provided further musical atmosphere from composer Andrew Howell. Its title and the music suggested something cosmic, or at least astronomical. Then the album came to a conclusion with "Genesis Ch.1 v.32." Woolfson was involved with writing every one of the songs, except for the Howell composition. Parsons assumed the role of director-producer. He recorded and engineered the tracks, assisted with arrangements, and produced the album.

The work of Parsons and Woolfson was acclaimed by Stephen Holden in *The Village Voice* on August 29, 1977. In his article, "Alan Parsons' Robot: Sci-Fi Cinerama," he observed the album's theme. The decline of man "came with the discovery of the wheel" said the liner notes. "I flinched when I read it," Holden wrote. But the theme was not pretentious, he concluded. He called *I Robot* "the head album of the year. While it offers warnings about humanity's imminent technological self-destruction," he wrote, it stands as "a stunning demonstration of its creator's control over technology": This is "massive, richly textured music," Holden said. He insisted that *I Robot* reflects our culture's "love-hate relationship with technology." Holden then added his view that Alan Parsons is responsible "for some of the grandest montage in rock." He referred to their music as "Mahlerian." *I Robot* lyrics are "based on a riddle rather than a narrative idea," he suggested. Parsons and Woolfson had achieved a remarkable fusion of their talents. Holden wrote: "But the scope of the sound is so majestic and the melody to graceful that mysticism eclipses dread." He asserted that "Breakdown" can stand next to the Who's *Tommy*, and he noted that the Alan Parsons Project recognizes and refers to R&B influences on "I Wouldn't Want to Be Like You."[3]

Certainly, the image of the robot has developed across the years, even as robots themselves have further developed. They have been tools and slave labor, or service robots that can take over human work functions. However, androids and cyborgs imitate human functions and develop toward artificial intelligence. That is, they transcend the capacity to perform assigned work tasks and begin to imitate human consciousness. Computers and robots merge to become artificial forms that may appear humanlike. Some science fiction writers have pushed this further, suggesting that all human functions are to be replaced by advanced robots. Bill Gates told Charlie Rose on PBS in February 2016 that he believes that robotics and computerization will advance to exceeding human capacity in about fifty years.

Robots force us to think about what it means to be human. What happens when a computer chip is inserted into a person, or an individual is reconstituted by technology to become the six million dollar man? What is an artificial person? What will happen if studies in artificial intelligence at MIT, or other research facilities in technological innovation, produce robots with keen artificial intelligence? As medical technology and computer technology advance, these questions, once posed by science fiction, arise more often and have to be taken quite seriously. As the public is given films like *AI: Artificial Intelligence* and *Ex Machina*, the inquiry into artificial intelligence by scientists proceeds like a mythical quest into the unknown.

The mythological ancestor of the robot is Talos, the giant that

Jason and the Argonauts must contend with as they seek the Golden Fleece. Talos is made of bronze and he guards the island of Crete. In the 1963 film *Jason and the Argonauts*, Talos creaks, like a door on a rusty hinge. He is a monstrous figure with sword in his hand and with his feet on the rocks on either side of the passageway through which the Argonauts must travel. This figure of Talos is decidedly mechanical.

Robots, however, have increasingly been conceived of as something beyond mechanical creatures of human invention. The modern idea of a robot appeared in Czechoslovakian writer Karel Capek's 1920 play *R.U.R.*: initials that designated Rossum's University Robots. These were organic beings, rather than mechanical ones. They were made from living tissue at the Rossum factory. These robots would serve mankind as cheap labor. However, in Capek's story they become more advanced and revolt, killing the humans, except for one. Fritz Lang's film *Metropolis* (1927) followed with an image of a robot. In 1938, Lester Del Rey created a domestic robot in his story "Helen O'Loy." Her name is derived from the metal alloys used to construct her. Two characters in the story want to find a way to humanize her and they succeed. She falls in love with one of them. O'Loy becomes a housewife in a marriage and the fact that she is a robot is hidden from view. When her husband dies she asks his friend to dismantle her and bury her with him.

Soon afterward, Isaac Asimov was writing his stories featuring robots. He asserted that robotics could develop in ways genuinely beneficial to humanity. He wrote *I, Robot, The Naked Sun, Caves of Steel* and featured some robots with humanlike qualities. The robots of Asimov are efficient, sometimes brilliant, and well-governed. They show robots as a positive benefit to mankind, in contrast with the labor-rebellion of Capek's robots, who ultimately threaten humanity. These images circulated through dozens of science fiction stories and became familiar figures in television and film. Helper robots were introduced to children in the 1960s on the television program *Lost in Space*, which featured a loveable robot who signaled any threat with a cry of "Danger, danger Will Robinson." In Ira Levin's 1972 satire *The Stepford Wives* (and its 2004 film remake) speculation arises that the women in a Connecticut community are robots. The robot as potential enemy, which hearkens back to the alienated creature of Mary Shelley's *Frankenstein*, can be seen in the robots and computers of the television series *Battlestar Gallactica* (2004) that would take over humanity, or in the cybernetic organism played by Arnold Schwartzenegger in James Cameron's film The *Terminator* (1984). The robots that appear in Asimov novels suggest a helper, more like C3PO and R2D2 in *Star Wars*.

Asimov's laws of robotics in *I, Robot* (1950) became a standard that other science fiction writers responded to: A robot must not injure a human being. A robot must obey orders given to it by human beings except when such orders conflict with the First Law to not harm human beings. A robot is required to protect itself while not violating either of the first two laws. Science fiction writer Stanislaw Lem opposed this view and stated that Asimov's laws of robots "give us a wholly false picture of the real possibilities."[4]

Eye in the Sky: *Surveillance and Telepathy*

Parsons and Woolfson followed *I Robot* with *Pyramid* (1978) and *Turn of a Friendly Card* (1980). With *Pyramid*, they imagined Egyptian mythology. *Turn of a Friendly Card* emerged from their time in Monaco and their fascination with the world of gambling. On the title song they explore the human tendency toward greed. The song is developed in five parts and features vocals by Chris Rainbow. The ballad "Time," with Eric Woolfson's vocal, is the closest thing to science fiction of the six songs offered on this album. "Games People Play," the album's other single, is sung by Lenny Zakatek. A reference to Edgar Allan Poe slips back into the picture with "The Gold Bug," an instrumental.

The Alan Parsons Project burst into full public view with their best-selling *Eye in the Sky* (1982), of which millions of copies have been sold. For this album they borrowed a title from a 1957 novel by Philip K. Dick and explored a dystopian world of surveillance. Woolfson was an avid science fiction reader but because of copyright he never took anything from either Asimov or Dick other than the general atmosphere of science fiction. Instead, he created his own narrative and set it to harmonic, smooth music that seemed much less edgy than the topics he had chosen. The clear, crisp, almost crystalline mastering of *I Robot* by Woolfson, produced with his daughter Sally and with Parsons, is a sign of the perfectionism in another musical era. "Nucleus" makes use of analog keyboards, a precursor to 1980s digital sampling, layering chords upon chords to create its distinctive sound. Their film-like music and radio friendly singles marked them as a progressive art band that recorded concept albums deeply identifying with science fiction.

Eye in the Sky (1982) opens with the spacey instrumental "Sirius." The popular distribution of the title song, "Eye in the Sky," which reached #3 of the Billboard charts, brought attention to the album's opening piece. "Sirius" has been used by the Chicago Bulls basketball team, when announcing its players before a game. The bass keeps playing at the end of this instrumental and brings us into the title track. "Eye in the Sky" may be about satellites, or about hidden cameras in a casino. The narrator may be spying on his lover, or the song may suggest Orwell's *1984* theme of "big brother is watching you." For some listeners today the lyric might anticipate more recent concerns about government monitoring of Internet use and phone conversations, given increased concerns about terrorism. The lyrics to "Eye in the Sky" speak not only of looking at someone but also about being able to read someone's mind. Thus, the song carries the suggestion of telepathy, which has remained a persistent theme in science fiction.[5]

"Children of the Moon" follows, with a choir, string and brass orchestration, and David Paton's vocals. The song continues a vaguely science fiction theme on this album. Yet, it soon becomes clear that with this record the Alan Parsons Project was moving away from the concept album approach. A suggestion of science fiction remains and a sense of mystery still lingers in the ethereal vocals. "Gemini" follows, with a title that may call up associations with space travel and the cosmos and the evocative vocal by Chris Rainbow. The symphonic effects by Parsons on "The Silence" and the 95 orchestral pieces conducted by Andrew Powell have a quality of airiness and suggest an expansiveness of space. This last song on the first side of the vinyl LP begins and ends with a ballad sung by Eric Woolfson. Its center is filled with Powell's rich orchestration. If one is listening to a CD remix of the album "The Silence" easily transitions into "You're Gonna Get Your Fingers Burned" and Lenny Zakotek's vocals. "Psychobabble" follows with a strong bass line and vocals from Elmer Gantry (Dave Terry). "Psychobabble" is energetic and pulses forward. In his review of the album Stephen Thomas Erlewine described the song as having "a bright propulsive edge."[6] "Mammogamma," which follows, was created on and by computers. "Step by Step" features a guitar solo from Ian Bainston. On this song a guitar is played directly into the mixing deck with no amplification. Zakotek contributes the vocal. "Old Wise" concludes the album. *Eye in the Sky* drew comparisons from critics with the work of 10CC, an English pop/rock band of producer-songwriters with an art-rock sensibility. Erlewine compared "Children of the Moon" to "Heart to Heart" by Kenny Loggins. He added the often repeated view that this album is not about a theme but is focused upon creating "a lushness of sound" with "sweet melody," textures and pop hooks.

The hit song "Eye in the Sky" may be about surveillance. However, it also raises the topic of telepathy with its lyric about reading one's mind. Telepathy makes group mind possible. "Most group mind stories, for instance, suggest the appearance of group mind is a function of the dynamics of evolution," writes Stan McDaniel.[7] He notes *Childhood's End* by Arthur C. Clarke as an example. He refers to the orthogenetic view of Teilhard de Chardin, which would not require telepathy. Teilhard coined the term *noogenesis* for mental evolution.[8] Teilhard de Chardin wrote: "The more complex a being is the more it is centered in itself and therefore the more conscious does it become."[9] The priest-paleontologist asserted that matter and life itself is a dynamic process emerging within consciousness and that the orientation of the evolutionary axis of development can be empirically determined.

Olaf Stapledon's *Last and First Men* (1930) presented a group mind of 96 individuals. In the story we read that this would not be possible "did not the temperament and capacity of each differ appropriately from those of the others."[10] Stapledon identifies evolutionary advancement with brain size but beyond past biological limits he posits the idea of group mind. The telepathic connection does not constitute group mind but a mode of association. In Clarke's *Childhood's End* first language must be removed. Clarke's narrator says that the group mind "will be a single entity as you yourselves are the sums of myriad cells."[11] In *Strangers in a Strange Land*, Robert A. Heinlein suggests group mind will be better than what came before it.

Musical Theatre

When Woolfson left Parsons to pursue musical theatre the Alan Parsons Project went into suspended animation for a few years. Woolfson began pursuing writing musicals with *Freudiana* (1990), which was based upon the life and works of Sigmund Freud. His songs from this became the basis for the last Alan Parsons Project recording. Parsons returned with of his own three songs, two of which were science fiction themed. Ian Bairnson and Stuart Elliott worked out the songs for *Time Machine* (1999). Professor Frank Close, an Oxford based physicist, narrates on the idea of the universe on "Temporalis." Dr. Close is a noted particle physicist who has served as vice-president of the British Association for the Advancement of Science and has been awarded the Kelvin Medal of the Institute of Physics for his contributions, through many books, lectures, and interviews, to public understanding of physics.

Through all of the years that they recorded as the Alan Parsons Project the group members never played live in concert. Parsons made up for that during the 1990s as he started a touring band and played music that has been described as by some rock music critics as symphony-rock. Woolfson was involved in the creation of *On the Air* (1996), which was about flight, from Daedelus and Icarus to the Apollo mission's flight in space. *On the Air* (1996), recorded by Parsons, was followed by *The Time Machine* (1999), an album using the title of H.G Wells's classic novel.

Woolfson's second musical, *Gaud*, was staged at Aachen, Germany, in 1994. The play went on to Alsdorf in 1995 and to Cologne in 1996. *Gambler* (1996) recalls the time he lived in Monte Carlo and utilizes songs from *Turn of a Friendly Card*, *Eye in the Sky*, and other Alan Parsons Project albums. *Dancing Shadows* (2007) was based upon a Korean play, *A Forest Fire*, and it played to audiences in South Korea. With his next musical, *Poe*, the songwriter revisited his interest in Edgar Allan Poe's works. He composed "Wings of Eagles," "Train to Freedom," and "Angel of the Odd," from a Poe story. The musical was staged at the Abbey Road Studios with Steve Balsamo, Anna-Jane Casey, Juliet Caton, David Burt, and James Gillan. The Halle Opera House produced *Poe* in Germany from August 2009 to March 2011, a time during which Woolfson passed away.

In 2010 Parsons' band changed members and again transformed into a live band. Alan Parsons turned his considerable recording talents in the direction of electronica. His son Jeremy made significant contributions to the recording. *A Valid Path* featured David Gilmore of Pink Floyd. Alan Parsons has recently developed a series of informative recording arts videos that are narrated by actor Billy Bob Thornton. There is an accompanying book in which studio techniques are discussed. Meanwhile, Parsons has worked with Lichtmond, a German electronic band and recorded ukulele player Jake Shimabukoro. He has contributed vocals to a recording project by Billy Sherwood and Chris Squire of Yes and he sang with Mexican pop music performer Aleks Syntek. The science fiction motifs that were such an important aspect of the Alan Parsons Project have faded into the past. The songs remain, with their richly produced sound and their images of robots and an eye in the sky.

Coda

Since David Bowie released his song "Changes" in January 1972 rock music has gone through many changes, breakthroughs, and reinventions. The mythic imagination has always stayed alive amid the transitions of culture and Bowie was one of rock's great experimenters with its possibilities. Bowie's passing in January 2016 was yet one more change. As a central figure in any discussion of rock, myth, and science fiction, he appears as one of those key performers whose work and mutating image may be called postmodern. His art, often in conversation with myth and with science fiction, was one of mime, theatre, and visual expression as well as one of music. On almost anyone's list of science fiction rock songs, Bowie's songs appear at the top. He made of himself a mythical figure. Bowie was involved in efforts to represent alienation, stardom, and culture through a play of signs that included science fiction imagery.[1] David Bowie was a rock cultural icon who played with myth.

Rock's devotion to the mythical may remind us that mythic imagination is ever at play in contemporary culture: in our art, our politics, our public rituals, and our entertainment. Postmodern fantasy, play, and the fusion of media (including rock music, print, and visuals) have an affinity with popular cultural forms, including the science fiction we see in films and on our TV screens. Science fiction is alive and well across print, electronic, and recorded media. In connection with rock music, science fiction offers open-ended, genre-bending possibilities. Gerald Alva Miller reminds us that "science fiction extrapolates beyond our present condition to imagine the potential transcendence of those limits."[2] Science fiction enables us to see things anew. It "destabilizes our normal conceptions of reality" and "inserts the marvelous into our reality," observes Miller. Consequently, our sense of stability may "prove to be nothing more than fantasies."[3] This has been the underlying message of rock songs and performances from artists like Bowie, Pink Floyd, Rush, or Iron Maiden. Creativity casts the world in new ways.

Rock music fantasy also calls to mind cyberpunk's recent ventures. Larry McCaffrey has connected the postmodernist philosopher Jean Baudrillard's thought with cyberpunk and he has proposed that technological changes can be linked with the postmodern condition. McCaffrey observes that artists who are "instinctively or intuitively" aware of this "have relied on themes and aesthetic modes previously associated with [science fiction]."[4] Rock music artists seem to have this instinctive response. Carlen Lavigne has pointed out that cyberpunk addresses technological issues in society. There are few aliens, space battles, or foreign planets in this fiction. Rather, there is attention to post-industrial society. She quotes science fiction writer Bruce Sterling's assertion that cyberpunk in the 1980s recognized social issues: "Technical culture has gotten out of hand," Sterling asserted." The advances of the sciences are so deeply radical, so disturbing, upsetting, and revolutionary that they can no longer be contained. They are surging into culture at large."[5] This surge of science into the culture is captured imaginatively in science fiction novels, films, television shows, and rock songs.

Despite all the dire observations of the music industry's decline in our digital age, rock music is very much alive. Rock music is fun. It is expressive play. Rock music speaks to us in a visceral way and it is not always as serious as a critic might make it seem. Rock is seriously expressive. When marketed, it becomes seriously commercial. Rock music was first theorized by practitioners rather than academics, by journalists, musicians, by record companies and their public relations departments, by radio producers and deejays. Rock criticism, as Simon Frith has said, is an investigation into a popular form of entertainment that is also "compelled to draw from high theory."[6] This reminds us that one of the features of postmodernism is the blending of high art and popular art. Like Frith, we can study material culture: how popular music is made, distributed, and consumed. But, also like Frith says, we also have to add that rock "in its mass cultural form" is engaged in "the struggle for fun."[7] Ultimately, reading science fiction and listening to rock music is about fun and imagination.

Coda

I hope that you have found some of this book fun and informative. Rock is to be welcomed as fun, even while it is subjected to criticism in the music press, by fans, or by others who choose to analyze its cultural impact. For anyone who pursues a study of rock music, myth, and science fiction further, listening is central. That is where you and I need to begin our interpretations. In *Rocking the Classics* Edward Macan observes: "Most popular music studies tend to be more sociologically than musicologically oriented."[8] This continues to be largely the case. Many early studies of rock focused on verbal messages in lyrics or on visuals rather than the music itself. Yet, to talk about music, as Luciano Pavorotti once observed, is like making love by chain mail. It is better to tune in with our feelings, to "be there," to listen and be moved.

Rock music manifests in culture and it offers fertile ground for cultural studies. Greil Marcus, for example, has brought rock into conversation with a consideration of American culture.[9] A critic like this offers keen perspectives on how rock speaks about our lives and our world. Likewise, we have much to gain from the inquiries and speculations of science fiction writers and critics. If we can still say that philosophy begins in wonder and seeks wisdom, they might be among the best popular thinkers of our time.

Science fiction has to contain some realism to appear rational and communicate with readers. Yet, it might be seen as a game "for grappling with issues of post-modern identity," as Gerald Alva Miller suggests.[10] This appears to be a feature of science fiction that David Bowie employed with his Ziggy Stardust persona and in testing the boundaries of gender and human identity. Science fiction of this sort, in Miller's words, destabilizes "our traditional definitions of self and society."[11] Miller reminds us that science fiction is a genre that allows us "to explore the human in new ways."[12] He points to Hayden White's emphasis upon narrative and White's view that story functions as humankind's most basic tool for making sense out of reality. Today we encounter "streams of data" that continually "emanate from media sources," he observes. To be human is to tell stories that "build our images of the world."[13]

Science fiction may speculate about the future. It may reflect the open-endedness and fragmentation in the postmodern condition. Critics note the genre's unique value. Science fiction looks at "material reducibility and at least implicitly, utopian possibility," observes Carl Freeman. Science fiction presents concepts that "have not yet been worked out," says Steven Shaviro. Miller describes science fiction as a space for "the fantastic, the marvelous, and the uncanny." Gary K. Wolfe points to science fiction's emergent literary respectability and a climate of increasing diversity.[14]

The appeal of science fiction for creative rock musicians and their audiences lies in its drive to know, its magic and drama, and its engagement with myth and the capacity for wonder. Readers and listeners are invigorated by the challenge of new and different worlds and characters. For Miller, "texts inscribe virtual spaces" and "science fiction is in a liminal space between realism and fantasy."[15] As reader response critics point out, the reader actualizes the text. Similarly, it is the listener to rock music who brings a song to life with his or her unique sensibility. So, with this coda, I encourage you to listen again and repeat that phrase. A listener like you, participating in the experience of music, is an interpreter of the sounds, patterns, and signs of a song. So, in an investigation of science fiction and myth in rock music, our best approach is to listen with open minds and hearts and to make up our own minds about the passionate, spacey, or mind-stretching sounds that we are hearing.

Chapter Notes

Introduction

1. See C.G. Jung, *The Collected Works of C.G. Jung*, Bollingen Edition (Princeton: Princeton University Press, 1970–1979).

2. Damien Cave, winter 1976.

3. Johannes Kepler, *Mysterium Cosmographum* (Tubingen, 1596, 2d ed., 1628).

4. Usula LeGuin, Introduction, *Norton Book of Science Fiction and Fantasy*, ed. Brian Attlebery and Ursula Le Guin (New York: Norton, 1997).

5. Robert Scholes is quoted by Raymond M. Olderman, *Beyond the Wasteland: A Study of the American Novel in the 1960s* (New Haven: Yale University Press, 1972), 26.

6. Mircea Eliade, Introduction, *Rites and Symbols of Initiation* (New York: Harper Torchbooks, 1965), ix.

7. Carl Sagan, *Cosmos* (Norwalk, CT: Easton), 196.

8. Joseph Campbell, *The Hero with Thousand Faces* (Princeton: Princeton University Press, 1949).

9. In his criticisms of rock music, Alan Bloom, in *The Closing of the American Mind* (1985), argued that rock was distracting the best and brightest of America from higher pursuits, like listening to Mozart, or the study of Plato. He called Mick Jagger of the Rolling Stones "Nietzsche's Nihiline." Bloom's concern was a variation on Plato, who would throw the poets out of his Republic and banish certain modes of music because of their presumably detrimental effect upon people and thus upon society. See Allan Bloom, *The Closing of the American Mind* (New York: Simon and Schuster, 1987).

10. Friedrich Nietzsche, Letter to Erwin Rohde, *Selected Letters of Friedrich Nietzsche*, trans. Anthony Ludovici (London: Heinemann, 1921, reprint 1923), 58.

11. Friedrich Nietzsche, *Works: The Birth of Tragedy from the Spirit of Music*, vol. I: 135–36.

12. *The Nation*, March 28, 1987: 16.

13. Norwood Russell Hanson suggests this in *Patterns of Discovery: An Inquiry into the Conceptual Foundations of Science* (Cambridge: Cambridge University Press, 1972).

14. Albert Einstein, *Ideas and Opinions (Mein Weltbild)*, trans., ed. Sonja Bargmann (Norwalk: Easton, 2004), 64–65.

Chapter One

1. See *Led Zeppelin and Philosophy*, ed. Scott Calef (Chicago: Open Court, 2009). Pop music listeners have heard of mythical places like Atlantis from Donovan and Avalon from Kenny Loggins. The mythical bird that rose from the ashes has appeared in "Phoenix" by Wishbone Ash and in the song and album *Phoenix* by Dan Fogelberg. In the mid–1970s listeners heard of the Celtic

moon-goddess of inspiration, night and death, "Rhiannon," from Fleetwood Mac. More recently radio pop brought Katy Perry's extraterrestrials and Lady Gaga's Venus.

2. Mike Pinder is quoted in Gary James's interview, www.classicbands.com.

3. Denny Laine was a member of Paul McCartney and Wings in the 1970s.

4. Mike Pinder interview with Gary James, www.classicbands.com.

5. Leon Hendrix and Adam Mitchell, *Jimi Hendrix: A Brother's Story* (New York: Thomas Dunne, 2012). Michael Moorcock's "Dead Singers" revives Jimi Hendrix (*Factions*, ed. Giles Gordon and Alexander Hamilton, 1974). See Michael Moorcock, *Book of Martyrs*, 1976. See also Gregory Benford, "Doing Lennon" *Analog* (April 1975) and Michael Swanwicj, "The Feast of St. Janis," *New Dimensions* 11 (1980).

6. Ian Abrahams, *Hawkwind: Sonic Assassins* (London: SAF, 2004).

7. C. Clerk, *The Saga of Hawkwind* (London: Omnibus, 2004).

8. Clerk, 8.

9. Edward Macan, *Rocking the Classics* (Oxford and New York: Oxford University Press, 1997), 41.

10. Abrahams, 83.

11. Abrahams, 38.

12. This included Moorcock's appearance on Hawkwind's *Earth Ritual* tour in 1984.

13. With Hawkwind in mind, M. Butterworth wrote science fiction novels *The Time of the Hawklords* (1976) and *Queens of Deliria* (1977) that depict the survival of a nuclear holocaust. The enemy attempt to affect the minds of the survivors by playing them the music of the Carpenters, Elton John, and Simon and Garfunkel.

14. Macan, *Rocking the Classics*, 73.

15. The Moody Blues produced no studio albums from 1972 to 1978.

16. Marianne Tatom Letts, *Radiohead and the Resistant Concept Album:*

How to Disappear Completely (Bloomington: Indiana University Press, 2010), 19. Hawkwind's psychedelia preceded the formation of Radiohead. Letts points to the use of Mellotron and Moog on Radiohead's *OK Computer* and calls the album one of "enormous scope," noting its artwork and its "dense subject matter."

17. Letts, 22.

18. Macan, 60.

19. Macan, 63.

20. Macan, *Endless Enigma: A Musical Biography of Emerson, Lake, and Palmer* (Chicago: Open Court, 2006), 59.

21. See Marianne Tatom Letts's discussion of concept albums in *Radiohead and the Resistant Concept Album*.

22. Letts, 14.

23. Yet, one may wonder if the Beatles album has the same "tonal and motivic coherence" that Shaugn O'Donnel hears on Pink Floyd's *The Dark Side of the Moon*. The Beatles' *Sgt. Pepper* recording comes under some scrutiny in Letts' discussion of concept albums. Letts considers the cohesive unity ascribed to the songs as perhaps "a function of commerce" (Letts, 17).

24. Macan, 59.

25. Macan, 60

26. Macan, 61.

27. Macan, 4.

28. Brian Stableford, *Science Fact, Science Fiction* (London: Routledge, 2006), 316.

29. For Edward Macan, as for Davin Seay and Mary Neely, the counterculture was religious or spiritually oriented. It was not primarily an ideological or oppositional movement. As Macan puts it, this "mirrored a generation's quest for some metaphysical depth" (*Rocking the Classics*, 6).

30. Macan, *Rocking the Classics*, 4.

31. John J. Scheinbaum, "Progressive Rock and the Inversion of Musical Values," in *Progressive Rock Reconsidered*, ed. Kevin Holm Hudson (London and New York: Routledge, 2002), 21–42.

32. Robert Walser's discussion appears in *Running with the Devil: Power, Gender, and Madness in Heavy Metal Music* (Middleton, CT: Wesleyan University Press, 1993). Walser examines the correlation between classical music and guitar solos by Ritchie Blackmore, Eddie Van Halen, and Randy Rhoades. In *Endless Enigma*, Edward Macan investigates the relationships between classical repertoire and the music of Emerson, Lake, and Palmer.

33. Andy Greene, "William Shatner on His New Prog Rock Album and *Star Trek*," *Rolling Stone*, September 11, 2013. Also see Tony Kaye, Rick Tierney, Scott Connor, *Spoken Word*.

34. Paul R. Kohl, review of Edward Macan, *Endless Enigma: A Musical Biography of Emerson, Lake and Palmer* (Chicago: Open Court, 2006).

35. Macan, *Endless Enigma*, 648.

36. Macan, *Endless Enigma*, 164.

37. Macan, *Endless Enigma*, 196.

38. Macan, *Endless Enigma*, 198.

39. Macan, *Endless Enigma*, 33.

40. Macan, *Endless Enigma*, 24.

41. Rick Wakeman and Marin Roach, *Grumpy Old Rock Star and Other Wondrous Stories* (London: Preface, 2008), 47.

42. Wakeman and Roach, 41.

43. Bill Martin, *Music of Yes: Structure and Vision in Progressive Rock* (Chicago: Open Court, 1997), 133.

44. Bill Martin, 134.

45. Stuart Chambers, *Yes: An Endless Dream of '70s, '80s, '90s Rock Music* (London: General Store Publication House, 2002), 135–36. Also see Interview with Steve Howe, www.bondgezou.com.

46. Jennifer Rycenga, 148. See "Tales of Change Within the Sound" in Kevin Holm-Hudson, *Progressive Rock Reconsidered* (London and New York: Routledge, 2002).

47. Paul Myers, *A Wizard, a True Star: Todd Rundgren in the Studio* (London: Jawbone, 2010), 118.

48. Myers, 140. The record includes "Space War." David Bowie attended Utopia's concert at Carnegie Hall and Neal Peart of Rush attended several shows (126).

49. Brian May's first band was named *1984*, after George Orwell's novel.

50. Brian May interview with Terry Gross, "Queen Guitarist Rocks Out to Physics," *The Guardian*, August 3, 2010, www.theguardian.com.

51. See Brian May, *Bang! The Complete History of the Universe* (London: Carlton, 2006).

52. May interview with Terry Gross, *The Guardian*, www.theguardian.com.

53. See Harris M. Berger's Foreword to the 2014 edition of Robert Walser, *Running with the Devil* (Middleton: Wesleyan University Press, 1993), vii.

54. Berger, xx.

55. Deena Weinstein also points to the apocalyptic strain of Christianity, especially *Revelation in Heavy Metal: The Music and Its Culture* (New York: Da Capo, 2000), 129.

56. Berger, vii.

57. Walser, 1.

58. Walser, 3–4.

59. Walser, 6–7. Robert Walser quotes Dickinson, 7.

60. Weinstein, 124. William Blake, in one of his poems, had a similar argument with the priests who exhausted all of the wonder and mystery from the garden.

61. Walser, 14.

62. Weinstein, 38.

63. Weinstein, 39.

64. Weinstein points to Van Halen's "Running with the Devil," Judas Priest's "Saints in Hell," AC/DC's "Highway to Hell" and "Sin City" among others. She notes how Iron Maiden made use of Poe's "Murders in the Rue Morgue" and how creators of heavy metal have drawn upon horror films, 40.

65. Weinstein, 40–41.

66. Robert Palmer, "Dark Metal: Not Just Smash and Thrash," *New York Times*, November 1990. See Weinstein, 43.

67. Chris Welsh interview with Jimmy Page, www.therockbackpages.com/ article.

68. Theodore Gracyk, *Listening to Popular Music: Or, How I Learned to Stop Worrying and Love Led Zeppelin* (Ann Arbor: University of Michigan Press, 2007), 32.

69. Chris Welsh interview with Jimmy Page. Mick Wall, *When Giants Walked the Earth: A Biography of Led Zeppelin* (London: Orion, 2008), 263.

70. Theodore Schick, *Led Zeppelin and Philosophy: All Will Be Revealed*, ed. Scott Calef (Chicago: Open Court, 2009), 97.

71. Susan Fast, *In the Houses of the Holy: Led Zeppelin and the Power of Rock Music* (Oxford: Oxford University Press, 2001), 50.

72. Fast, 50.

73. Fast, 52, 57.

74. Fast, 52.

75. Fast, 53.

76. *Ibid.*

77. See *Led Zeppelin and Philosophy*, 105–09. "Achilles Last Stand" is on *Presence* (1976).

78. Randall E. Auxier, "Magic Pages and Mythic Plants," 117–27, Calef, *Led Zeppelin and Philosophy*, 118.

79. Auxier, 127.

80. Auxier, 123.

81. Fast, 54, 56.

82. Fast, 50, 56.

83. Calef, *Led Zeppelin and Philosophy*, 136–39.

84. Martin Popoff says the tuning down began with the album *Master of Reality, Black Sabbath: Doom Let Loose* (Toronto: ECW, 2006), 57.

85. Walser, 148.

86. Deena Weinstein notes that some heavy metal lives in the same universe as tabloid news and the "prole" leanings of fans of pro wrestling, 294. Black metal was heard in Norway in the 1990s with Burzum and Mayhem. It featured keyboards as well as guitar, bass, and drums, piercing vocals, and visuals that called upon an array of Western imagery representing the demonic. A disturbing byproduct of black metal was the burning of old churches or the desecration of cemeteries.

Chapter Two

1. C.G. Jung, *The Theory of Psychoanalysis and Integration of the Personality*. In his study of symbols, Carl Jung was "grappling with the endless proliferation of mythical fantasies" (*Symbols*, Part II, 220). In 1934, Dr. Joseph Henderson observed a trend in Jung's work. Deirdre Baer writes: "There is a clear, discernible trend in his writings from mid-decade onward, as he recounts fewer and fewer of his patients' personal problems and his own technical methods of dealing with them. More and more, he directs his attention toward the non-personal, the objective, the psychic, and all those concepts he would eventually gather under the rubric of the 'archetypes of the collective unconscious,'" Deirdre Baer, *Jung: A Biography* (New York and Boston: Little, Brown, 2003), 395.

2. Jenny Boyd and Holley George Warren, *Musicians in Tune*, New York: Fireside, 120.

3. Jung writes: "The forms we use for assigning meaning are historical categories that reach back into the mists of time" (*Collected Works*, 9.1: 32–33). Archetypes have potential that is actualized when engaged within a particular culture and time. See Joseph Campbell, "Imprints of Experience," *Primitive Mythology: The Masks of Gods* (Princeton: Princeton University Press, 1973), 50–131.

4. Deena Weinstein, 214. Weinstein cites Aldous Huxley's comments on theatre, in which lighting and effects bring spectators into that "other world, which lies at the back of every mind, however perfect its adaptation to the exigencies of social life, 217. Aldous Huxley, *The*

Doors of Perception and Heaven and Hell, 165.

5. Weinstein, 214–15.

6. Weinstein 232; Durkheim, *The Elementary Forms of Religious Life*, 470.

7. Weinstein, 232.

8. Ernst Cassirer, *An Essay on Man* (New Haven: Yale University Press, 1944, reprint 1967), 32.

9. Cassirer, 73.

10. Cassirer, 25.

11. Cassirer, 27.

12. William J. Broad, *The Oracle: The Lost Secrets and Hidden Message of Ancient Delphi* (New York: Penguin, 2006), 13. See Anthony De Curtis, "Myth and Commerce in the Music Business," in *Stars Don't Stand in the Sky: Music and Myth* (New York: New York University Press, 1999), 32.

13. David Buckley, *Strange Fascination, David Bowie: The Definitive Story* (London: Virgin, 1999), 60. Buckley notes that Bowie talked with producer Tony Visconti about "Bradbury, Asimov and Sturgeon, as well as some obscure writers," including the Julian Jaynes book. See *Strange Fascination*, 60.

14. For other examinations of creativity, you might consult the work of psychologist Frank Barron. See also Brewster Ghiselin, *The Creative Process* (1952) and Rollo May, *The Courage to Create* (New York: Norton, 1993).

15. Erich Fromm, *The Forgotten Language of Dreams, Fairy Tales and Myth* (New York: Grove, 1951).

16. Robert Walser, *Running with the Devil: Power, Gender, and Madness in Heavy Metal Music* (Middleton, CT: Wesleyan University Press, 1993), 108. Examples of the uses of myth in classical art music are numerous. Orpheus appears in Monteverdi *L'orfeo* (1607); Christoph Gluck, *Orpheus Ed Euridice* (1763); and Jacques Offenbach, *Orphee Aux Enfers* (Orpheus and the Underworld). We meet the story of Troy in Hector Berlioz's *Les Troyens* (1858), a five-act opera. Virgil's *Aenead* appears in Henry Purcell's

Dido and Aeneas (1689). Also notable is Mozart's *Ideomeneo* (1781). Richard Straus wrote many operas with mythic settings: *Elektra* (1909), *Ariadne and Naxos* (1912), *Die a Gypsche Helena* (1927), *Daphne* (1938).

17. T.S. Eliot, "Tradition and Individual Talent," (1919) in *The Sacred Wood*. London: Faber and Faber 1923. *Selected Essays*, New York: Harcourt Brace, 3–11.

18. Leigh Brackett, Introduction to *The Best of Planet Stories*, vol. 1 (New York: Random House, 1975).

19. Paul F. Ford, *Companion to Narnia: A Complete Guide to the Magical World of C.S. Lewis' Narnia* (New York: HarperCollins, 2005), 295.

20. John Cawelti, *Six Gun Mystique* (Bowling Green: Bowling Green University Press, 1999), 31.

21. Joseph Campbell and Bill Moyers, *The Power of Myth* (New York: Anchor, 1991), 183.

22. Mircea Eliade, *Myth and Reality*, trans. Willard Trask (New York: Harper Torchbooks, 1968), 141.

23. Neil Peart interview, June 13, 2012, *The Objective Standard*, www.the objectivestandard.com.

24. Herbert Wells, in *H.G. Wells, the Critical Heritage*, ed. Patrick Parrinder (London: Routledge, Kegan, Paul, 1972), 260.

25. See Nicholas Pegg, *David Bowie* (London: Reynolds and Acorn, 2002; reprint, London: Titan, 2011).

26. *Los Angeles Times*, September 1974.

27. Wendy Leigh, *Bowie: The Biography* (London and New York: Gallery, 2014), 15.

28. Buckley, 39.

29. Gary K. Wolfe, *The Known and the Unknown: The Iconography of Science Fiction* (Kent State: Kent State University Press, 1979), 15.

30. C.S. Lewis, *Of Other Worlds: Essays and Stories*, ed. Walter Hooper and Geoffrey Bles (London: Bles, 1966), 111–12. Hard science fiction has focused

upon rigorous and accurate scientific findings and technical details. It is one way of categorizing science fiction stories. Asimov's short story "Evidence" is one example.

31. Ursula Le Guin, Introduction, *Norton Book of Science Fiction* (New York: Norton, 1997).

32. Leigh Brackett is cited by Rosemary Arbur, 11.

33. Alfred I. Tauber, *Science and the Quest for Meaning* (Waco: Baylor University Press, 2009), 139. Tauber writes that science acts upon presuppositions: the view that "The world is material and ordered; we might discern this order by detached empirical observation, neutral rational description, and objective analysis; laws will emerge from this inquiry and they will remain inviolable; why nature corresponds to our human mathematical and objective descriptions remains mysterious, but the empirical product of that method has been highly successful and thus approximates a depiction of the real as truth," 218, n. 4.

34. Walser, 26.

35. Pat Cadigan, *Ultimate Cyberpunk*, x. The term cyberpunk originated from a 1985 *Washington Post* article by Gardner Dazois who drew the term from the title of Bruce Bethke's 1983 short story "Cyberpunk." See Carlen Lavigne's excellent study: *Cyberpunk Woman, Feminism and Science Fiction: A Critical Study* (Jefferson, NC: McFarland, 2013).

36. Richard Maltby views popular culture as "Escapism that is not an escape from or to anywhere, but an escape of our utopian selves," 14.

37. *Ibid.*

38. Alvin Toffler, *Future Shock* (New York: Random House, 1970), 384.

39. Raymond Williams and Pierre Bourdieu, both cited in *Popular Culture*, 5.

40. Raymond Williams, analysis, in *Popular Culture*, 32.

41. Williams, 36.

42. Wolfe, 13.

43. Samuel R. Delany, *The Jewel Hinged Jaw* (New York: Berkeley Windhover, 1978). See Nicholas D. Smith, *Philosophers Look at Science Fiction* (London: Burnham, 1982), 12.

44. Michael Berman, *Everyday Fantastic: Essays on Science Fiction and Human Being* (Cambridge: Cambridge University Press, 2008), 18.

45. Robert A. Heinlein, *Nature, Faults and Virtues*, 22. Heinlein's "Future History" series looks at potential problems in the future. "Universe and Common Sense" in *Astounding*, 1941.

46. William Atheling, Jr. (James Blish), *More Issues at Hand* (Chicago: Advent, 1970).

47. Joanna Russ, "Speculations: The Subjunctivity of Science Fiction," *Extrapolation* 15.1 (December 1973): 52.

48. See Henry Jenkins, "Strangers No More, We Sing: Filking and the Social Construction of the Science Fiction Fan Community," in Lisa A. Lewis, *The Adoring Audience: Fan Culture and Popular Media* (London: Routledge, 1992). This article explores consumers who also produce (212) and fan music making. Jenkins offers the example of *Star Trek* as fan culture, 214–16.

49. Stuart Hall and Paddy Wannel discuss the interactions between text and audience and social relations in popular music "youth" culture. They assert that exposure to the work contributes to the shape of one's mental image of the world, *The Popular Arts* (London: Hutchison, 1964), 281.

50. The signs that appear in connection with progressive rock, heavy metal, or other rock genres are rooted in culture. This semiology, Robert Walser points out, is best approached through ethnography, historical analysis, and argumentation about culture (31). Music is a social activity in which the use of myth and symbols can be productive of new meanings for listeners. An inquiry into this can help us to understand the consciousness, thoughts, desires, and

dreams of a culture and its rock-influenced subcultures (34).

51. Robert Scholes, *Structural Fabulation: An Essay on Fiction of the Future* (University of Notre Dame Press, 1975), 29. The fan of progressive rock, for example, knows codes to which the uninitiated are oblivious, observes Edward Macan in *Rocking the Classics* (Oxford: Oxford University Press, 1997).

52. See Brian Atteberg and Veronica Hollinger, *Parabolas of Science Fiction* (Middletown: Wesleyan University Press, 2013), 8. Samuel R. Delany uses the example of a huge red sun and a blue one (1978), 26.

53. William Tenn is the science fiction writing pseudonym for Philip Klass.

54. Atteberg and Hollinger, 9.

55. Science fiction offers us a way to overcome the separation of the two cultures of science and literature that was of concern when C.P. Snow delivered his Rede Lectures in 1959. Snow wrote at a time when science was still something of a cultural outsider. The study of science was then an intellectual pursuit that was only beginning to break into the curriculum at the British universities. Scientific study had first been offered at the "brick" universities in northern England and only later became part of the curriculum at Oxford and Cambridge.

56. Aldous Huxley was quite aware of J.B.S. Haldane's essay "Daedelus, or Science and the Future" (1923), in which Haldane wrote: "The scientific worker of the future will more and more resemble the lonely figure of Daedelus as he becomes conscious of his ghastly [enterprise] and proud of it" (London: Kegan Paul, 1923), 93.

57. Wolfe, 15.

58. Neil Gaiman, Foreword, Samuel R. Delany, *Einstein Intersection* (Middletown: Wesleyan University Press, 1998), vii.

59. Gaiman, viii, ix.

60. Larry McCaffrey, *Storming the Reality Studio* (Durham: Duke University Press, 1991), 3–4.

61. Scholes, 24. Robert Scholes begins his book writing about metafiction, or fiction that is about other fiction.

62. Kingsley Amis, *New Maps of Hell: A Survey of Science Fiction* (London: Gollancz, 1961), 54.

63. See Brian Aldiss's comments in the first chapter of *The Billion Year Spree: The True History of Science Fiction* (New York: Schocken, 1974). Aldiss points to sources in the Gothic novel and points out that Ann Radcliffe's *Mysteries of Udolpho* continually explained the apparently unnatural phenomena.

64. Aldous Huxley, Letter to Ketheran Roberts (May 18, 1931). *Letters of Aldous Huxley*, ed. Grover Smith (New York: Harper and Row, 1969).

65. Wolfe, 125.

66. Aldiss, *Billion Dollar*, 246–47. Gary K. Wolfe provides a list of some apocalyptic science fiction stories, 127.

67. Robert Bloch in Basil Davenport's symposium of the science fiction novel in 1959 called it an unconscious social criticism.

68. David Wragg, "Or Any Art at All: Frank Zappa Meets Critical Theory," *Popular Music* 20, no. 2 (May 2001): 217.

69. Michael Polyani and Harry Prosch, *Meaning* (Chicago: University of Chicago Press, 1975), 25. The Nobel Prize winning biologist Julian Huxley wrote: "It is the merest ant and twaddle to go on asserting, as most of our press and people continue to do, that increase of scientific knowledge and power must in itself be good" (238). See "The Tissue Culture King," *Time Probe: The Sciences in Science Fiction*, ed. Arthur C. Clarke.

70. Lewis Mumford, *The Pentagon of Power, The Myth of Machine* (New York: Harcourt, Brace, Jovanovich, 1974), 27.

71. Victor Ferkiss, *Technological Man: The Myth and Reality* (New York: New American Library, 1970), 255.

72. Dave Grohl and the Foo Fighters celebrate the musical character of American cities on their album *Sonic Highways* (RCA, 2014). In "Running on

Empty" (1978), Jackson Browne suggests that he and the band can't even remember which city they are in because they've done so many shows in a row.

73. Raymond Williams, *The Country and the City* (London: Chatto and Windus, 1973), 72–276.

74. Ketterer (102) is cited by Gary K. Wolfe, 86.

75. Theodore Roszak, *Where the Wasteland Ends* (Garden City, NY: Doubleday), 10.

76. Gary K. Wolfe, *How Great Science Fiction Works* (Chantilly, VA: The Great Courses, 2016), 169.

77. Wolfe, *How Great Science Fiction Works*, 105.

78. Wolfe, *How Great Science Fiction Works*, 88–91.

79. Wolfe makes these observations and cites parallels, *How Great Science Fiction Works*, 95.

80. Wolfe, *How Great Science Fiction Works*, 97.

81. See Raymond Williams, *The Country and the City*, 276–280.

82. Northrup Frye, *Anatomy of Criticism* (Princeton: Princeton University Press, 1957), 33. For this quote see "The Archetypes of Literature," *Kenyon Review* 1 (1951), 49. In *Anatomy of Criticism*, Frye connects myth and literary tradition intertextually and he does not refer to the collective unconscious as the source of archetypes in the Jungian sense. "Poetry Can Only Be Made Out of Other Poems; Novels Out of Other Novels" (97). The recurring images of archetypes are "Social Facts" that "Help to Integrate Our Literary Experience" (99). See George Jensen's discussion in *Post-Jungian Criticism: Theory and Practice* (Albany: SUNY Press, 2003), 6–7.

Chapter Three

1. "What united the Bay Area bands was their need to assimilate traditional American folk musics, particularly the blues, into rock" (Hall, 386). Ferdinand de Saussure provided the terms sign, signifier, and signified to describe how we use language. Roland Barthes held that myth is a system of communication. Semiotics is the study of meaning making through signs.

2. Richard King has referred to this countercultural sensibility as an effort "to create a new religion." See *The Party of Eros, Radical Social Thought and the Realm of Freedom* (Chapel Hill: University of North Carolina Press, 1972).

3. *Creem* (1974), 71. Variations on this theme have been provided by Coleman, 1992 (447), Considine (663), and Evans, 1992 (364). M. Coleman's reviews are on Barry Manilow, The Carpenters, Journey, and Neil Diamond. See Steve Jones, *Pop Music and the Press* (Philadelphia: Temple University Press, 1974).

4. See Simon Frith, *Sound Effects: Youth, Leisure, and the Politics of Rock and Roll* (London: Constable, 1983), 163. The notion that "Rock and roll has saved lives" is found in Marsh's biography of Bruce Springsteen, *Born to Run* (Introduction, xvi).

5. Ram Dass, *Be Here Now* (San Cristobal, NM: Lama Foundation, 1971). *Be Here Now* encourages presence in the moment.

6. Nancy Reid, "Clinging to the Edge of Magic: The Shamanic Aspects of the Grateful Dead," 183.

7. Reid, 184.

8. Reid, 185.

9. Graham Nash, *Wild Tales: A Rock and Roll Life* (New York: Crown, 2013), 199.

10. David Crosby and Carl Gottlieb, *Long Time Gone* (New York: Doubleday, 1988; reprint 2000), 19.

11. Nash, 204.

12. Nash, 120.

13. Nash, 186.

14. Nash, 199.

15. Michio Kaku, *Physics of the Impossible: A Scientific Exploration of Phasers, Force Fields, Teleportation and Time*

Travel (New York: Doubleday, 2008), 166.

16. Kaku, 169.

17. Kaku, 168.

18. Cited by Gary K. Wolfe, *The Known and the Unknown: The Iconography of Science Fiction* (Kent State: Kent State University Press, 1979), 22–23.

19. Wolfe, 21.

20. Wolfe, 74–75.

21. Marion Leonard points out that for some critics they both have a "tomboy image." Marion Leonard, *Gender in the Music Industry: Rock Discourse and Girl Power* (Aldershot: Ashgate, 2007), 37. There have been no science fiction references from Joan Jett, Laura Nyro, Patti Smith, Pat Benatar, Melissa Etheridge, or many other female rock performers. The B52s got as far as naming their band after a plane but no prominent female group has chosen an interstellar space vehicle to represent their band. It might be asked why female rock performers have not more extensively explored the science fiction medium as a resource for their work.

22. Patti Smith, *The Guardian* (May 2005).

23. This Lenny Kaye interview appears online.

24. Jenny Garber in *The Lost Women of Rock Music: Female Musicians in the Punk Era*, ed. Helen Reddington (Aldershot: Ashgate, 2007), 3.

25. Mircea Eliade, *Myth and Reality*, trans. Willard Trask (New York: Harper Torchbooks, 1968), 417.

26. Eliade, 421.

27. Eliade, 421–22.

28. Eliade, 423.

29. Jones (99) offers a sampling of rock critics who address a preference for "tougher, grittier, more real," "intensity," and "passion over precision."

30. Kambrew McLeod, 108.

31. McLeod, 109. For example, Dave Marsh wrote of Neil Young's *Tonight's the Night* in 1975: "The music has a quality of offhand first take crudity matched recently only by *Blood on the Tracks*," 67.

32. Harding and Nett, 60. Gottlieb and Wald, 252. Norma Coates (1998), 79. Coates' comment "ultimately fictive masculinity" appears 52–53, "Revolution Now? Rock and the Political Potential of Gender," *Sexing the Gender: Popular Music and Gender*, ed. Sheila Whitely (London: Routledge, 1997). Coates' thoughts on "stereotypical masculinity" are on 52. Mimi Schippers, *Rockin' Out of the Box: Gender Manuvering in Alternative Hard Rock* (New Brunswick, NJ: Rutgers University Press, 2002), 23, see 20–23. Sheila Whitely suggests that songs present the evil woman who ruins men's lives, *The Space Between the Notes: Rock and Counterculture* (London: Routledge, 2000), 38; Deena Weinstein, *Heavy Metal Music and Culture* (New York: Da Capo, 2000), 104; Robert Walser, *Running with the Devil* (Middleton: Wesleyan University Press, 114–17).

33. Rock has focused on being accessible and commercial by centering attention on its well-known 'classic' performers connoting an aura of "Stability." Coates gives attention to *Rocklist* to demonstrate how the gendered list indicates the masculinist discourse of rock and "replicates the social dynamics currently operative in nascent cyberspace," 81.

Chapter Four

1. In January 1970 Carl Wayne left the Move. On July 12, 1970 Wood added strings to a Lynne song that was intended as a Move B-side. The Move's final album, *Message from the Country*, was finished. The song became the first ELO single.

2. This is the number of hits in the United States. ELO had 26 UK pop singles.

3. For the Special Theory of Relativity (1905) see Albert Einstein, "On the

Electrodynamics of Moving Bodies," *Annalen Der Physiks* 17 (1905): 801–921. For the General Theory of Relativity (1914–1915) see his November 1915 publications "On the Theory of General Relativity," "Explanation of the Perihelion Motion of Mercury," and "Field Equations on the Theory of Gravitation." Also of interest are Einstein's exposition of the hole argument in *Physikalishe Zeitschraft* 15 (1914), "On the Relativity Problem" *Scientia* 15 (1914): 337–48, and "The Formal Foundation of the General Theory of Relativity" (1914). "Contributions to Quantum Theory" (1914), "The Space-Time Problem," *Koralle* 5 (1930): 486–88. The papers, originally in German, are available in English translation.

4. Other ELO records include: *Balance of Power* and *Zoom*. Band members included Mike Edwards (cello), Andy Craig (cello), Hugh McDowell (cello), Wilfred Gibson (violin), Mike de Albuquerque (bass), Colin Walker (cello), Mik Kaminski (violin), Kelly Groucutt (bass and vocals), Dave Morgan (guitar, synthesizer, vocals) Melvyn Gale (cello), Louis Clark (synthesizers, string arranger).

5. Axl Rose was quick to distinguish hard blues oriented rock from pop music at this MTV gathering in 1992. Several critics, from Dave Marsh to Robert Christgau, have argued for "authentic" rock as blues based and different from pop music. ELO has only gradually redeemed itself from the pop category among some critics.

6. Intervals of music may be consonant. Pythagoras found that ratios of 2:1, 3:2, and 4:3 sound consonant. Major thirds, major sixths, and minor thirds are consonant. Hemholtz determined that musical dissonance occurs in the greatest when partials of two tones are at 30 to 40 beats per second.

7. Jeff Lynne, who worked with ELO's array of orchestral and rock instruments as the band's primary songwriter and producer, has earned wide recognition as a fine record producer for his efforts with other musicians.

Chapter Five

1. David Bowie, *Strange Fascination: David Bowie, the Definitive Biography* (London: Virgin, 1999), 160.

2. Gordon Coxkill, interview with David Bowie, in *Bowie on Bowie: Interviews and Encounters with David Bowie*, ed. Sean Egan (Chicago: Chicago Review Press, 2015), 11.

3. Interview with David Bowie, *Bowie on Bowie*, 167.

4. David Thompson, *Hallo Spaceboy: The Rebirth of David Bowie* (Toronto: ECW, 2006), 2.

5. Simon Frith and Howard Home, *Art into Pop* (London: Methuen, 1987). See also *Enchanting David Bowie: Space, Time, Body, Memory*, ed. Tonja Cinque, Christopher Moore, and Sean Redmond (London: Bloomsbury, 2015), 276.

6. Peter Doggett, *The Man Who Sold the World: David Bowie in the 1970s* (New York: HarperCollins, 2012), Introduction.

7. Christopher Lasch, *The Age of Narcissism: American Life in an Age of Diminishing Expectations* (New York: W.W. Norton, 1979).

8. Doggett, Introduction.

9. *Ibid.*

10. Buckley, 19.

11. Buckley, 60. Bowie discussed Julian Jaynes' *The Origins of the Bicameral Mind* with Tony Visconti. Bowie was an avid reader and his adult reading has been documented by the Art Gallery of Toronto, Ontario. His reading includes R.D. Laing's *The Divided Self*, the poetry of Allen Ginsberg, *On the Road* by Jack Kerouac, works by Martin Amis, Peter Ackroyd, William S. Burroughs, Julian Barnes, Bruce Chatwin, Stephen King, Don De Lillo's *White Noise*, Colin Wilson's *The Outsider*, and many others.

12. Buckley, 60–61.

13. See Paul Trynka, *Starman* (Boston and New York: Little, Brown, 2011), Chapter One. *The Day of the Triffids* was also broadcast by the BBC.

14. Marc Spitz, *Bowie: A Biography* (New York: Crown/Archetype, 2010), 22.

15. Wendy Leigh, *Bowie: The Biography* (London and New York: Gallery, 2014), 29.

16. David Bowie interview, *Los Angeles Times* (September 1974), in *Bowie on Bowie: Interviews and Encounters with David Bowie*, ed. Sean Egan (Chicago: Chicago Review, 2015).

17. Michael Mooradian Lupro cites Ken McLeod (2003) and Taylor (2001). See "Keeping Space Fantastic: The Transformative Journey of Major Tom," *Enchanting David Bowie: Space, Time, Body, Memory*, ed. Toija Cinque, Christopher Moore, and Sean Redmond (London: Bloomsbury, 2015). Ken McLeod makes a reference to an internal space of "feelings, desires, dreaming" (337). Sheila Whiteley speaks of space as empowering. Bowie creates space sonically. Sheila Whiteley, *The Space Between the Notes: Rock Music and the Counterculture* (New York and London: Routledge, 1993), 3.

18. Richard Fitch, "In This Age of Grand Allusion: Bowie, Nihilism and Meaning," (19–34). *David Bowie, Critical Perspectives*, ed. Eoin Devereaux, Aileen Dillane, and Martin J. Power (London: Routledge, 2015).

19. Ellen Willis, *Out of the Vinyl Deeps: Ellen Willis on Rock Music* (Minneapolis: University of Minnesota Press, 2011).

20. The name of the record company, Trident, and the name of the space mission, Apollo, both recall figures from Greek mythology. So does the name of the Trident studio in which the album was recorded: a name associated with the pitchfork of Poseidon/Neptune, the god of the sea.

21. Carmen Paglia's observation comes three years earlier than Don McLean's *American Pie* in which he sings of a generation lost in space. Wendy Leigh, *David Bowie: The Biography* (London: Gallery, 2014), 15. Van Cagle, *Reconstructing Pop/Subculture: Pop, Rock, and Andy Warhol* (Thousand Oaks and London: Sage 1995), 112. Philip Auslander, *Performing Glam Rock, Theatricality and Gender in Popular Music* (Ann Arbor: University of Michigan Press, 2006), 128. Michael Mooradian Lupro, "Keeping Space Fantastic: The Transformative Journey of Major Tom." Marc Spitz, *Bowie: A Biography* (New York: Crown/Archetype, 2010), 105–06.

22. Willis, 39.

23. Willis 38.

24. Willis, 39.

25. Doggett, 155.

26. Willis, 39.

27. "Beat Godfather Meets Glitter Main Man," William S. Burroughs' interview with David Bowie, *Rolling Stone*, February 28, 1974.

28. "Goodbye Ziggy and a Big Hello to Aladdin Sane," David Bowie interview with Charles Shaar Murray, *New Musical Express*, January 27, 1973. *Bowie on Bowie*, 31. Bowie commented in this interview that he admired John Lennon's ability to create puns.

29. Simon Frith, *Sound Effects: Youth, Leisure, and the Politics of Rock N' Roll* (New York: Pantheon, 1981), 154.

30. Simon Frith, "David Bowie," *Let It Rock*, June 1973.

31. Spitz, *Bowie: A Biography* (New York: Crown/Archetype, 2010), 39.

32. Carmen Paglia is quoted by Spitz, *Bowie: A Biography*, 39.

33. David Bowie interview, youtube.com, Broadcast Interviews, 1977.

34. Nicholas Pegg, *The Complete David Bowie* (London: Titan, 2011).

35. Simon Frith (1988, 136) is quoted by Ian Chapman in "Ziggy's Urban Alienation: Assembling the Heroic Outsider," *Enchanting David Bowie*.

36. Ian Chapman cites Richard Lehan, *The City in Literature* (Berkeley: University of California Press 1998), 98.

37. Raymond Williams, "The Metropolis and the Emergence of Modernism," in *Unreal City: Urban Experience in Modern European Literature and Art*, ed. David Kelley and Edward Timms (Manchester: Manchester University Press, 1985), 13–14, 23.

38. Christopher Booker, *The Seven Basic Plots: Why We Tell Stories* (New York: Continuum, 2004), 33.

39. Booker, 33. See Booker's discussion about science fiction, 39–45.

40. Gary K. Wolfe, 21.

41. Charles Shaar Murray interview with David Bowie, "David at the Dorchester," *Interviews and Encounters with David Bowie*, 16.

42. Interview with David Bowie, *Interviews and Encounters with David Bowie*, 31.

43. Gary K. Wolfe points out that in James Blish's story, *A Case of Conscience*, there is a catastrophe in which science has "swept away the theories that forbade" travel faster than light. "People on one side of a revolution may be quite incapable of understanding people on the other side" (Barker, 80–81).

44. Carl G. Jung, *Flying Saucers: A Modern Myth of Things Seen in the Sky*, trans. R.F.C. Hull (New York: Harcourt Brace, 1959), 10.

45. Bowie is quoted as saying that he would visually draw the direction of an instrumental solo. This one went from a flat line to sprays of broader lines. See *The Complete David Bowie* by Nicholas Pegg, under "Moonage Daydream."

46. James T. Jones, 236. Jones points out that literature helps us to experience abstract moral issues more concretely, 240. The novelist John Gardner echoes this view in *On Moral Fiction* (New York: Basic, 1978).

Chapter Six

1. Roy Shipston, "Are Spacemen Floyd on Their Way Back to Earth?" Interview with Pink Floyd, *Disc Maker Echo*, November 22, 1969, 59.

2. Shipston, 58.

3. Nicholas Schaffner, *Saucerful of Secrets: The Pink Floyd Odyssey* (New York: Dell, 1991), 35.

4. Julian Palocios, *Syd Barrett and Pink Floyd: Dark Globe* (London: Plexus, 2010), 110.

5. Palocios, 113–14.

6. In Barrett's song "Bike" he says the sound will "Ching." Barrett was familiar with the I Ching and was intrigued by his copy of Richard Wilhelm's translation of it. See Palocios, 111. On *The Dark Side of the Moon*, in "Time," clocks chime as the song begins and later we race toward a sinking sun only to have it arise behind us again.

7. Richard Cromelin, "Roger Waters: Dark Side of the Tube," *Los Angeles Times*, September 13, 1992. Also see Irwin Stambler, *Pop Rock Sound* (New York: St. Martin's, 1974), 400.

8. John Cavanaugh, *The Piper at the Gates of Dawn* (New York and London: Continuum, 2007). Cavanaugh tells his story of his first acquaintance with the song after coming indoors from a starry night. He begins his introduction with this recollection.

9. *Ibid.*

10. The "aura of science fiction and fantasy" around the band had led to "specialized gigs" such as one at an American science fiction convention," notes Nicholas Schaffner, *Saucerful of Secrets*, 136.

11. Syd Barrett released *The Madcap Laughs* (Harvest/Capitol, 1969). *Barrett* (1970) appeared the next year. There was also a record title *Opel* (1988). *The Madcap Laughs* was re-mastered in 2010.

12. Richard Middleton, "Piper at the Gates of Dawn," *Pop Music and the Blues* (1972). *Pink Floyd Through the Eyes of the Band, Its Fans, Friends and Foes*, ed. Bruno MacDonald (New York: Da Capo, 1997), 44.

13. Miles, *International Times* (July 1968): 46.

14. Mick Favreu, *International Times* (October 1969): 47. *Pink Floyd Through the Eyes of the Band, Its Fans, Friends, and Foes*, ed. Bruno MacDonald (New York: Da Capo, 1996), 44.

15. Shipston, 59.

16. Musicologist Lawrence Kramer has pointed out that interpretation cannot be controlled. It may reach toward "any association, substitution, analogy, construction, or leap of inference that it requires." Lawrence Kramer, *Music as Cultural Practice* (Berkeley: University of California, 1990), 15.

17. Robert Christgau, "Dark Side of the Moon," *Christgau's Record Guide: Rock Albums of the 70s* (Boston: Ticknor and Fields, 1989), 6.

18. John Harris, *Dark Side of the Moon: The Making of the Pink Floyd Masterpiece* (New York: Da Capo, 2006), 16.

19. Harris, Introduction.

20. Phil Rose, *Roger Waters and Pink Floyd: The Concept Albums* (Madison: Fairleigh Dickinson University Press, 2015). Waters made this comment in an interview with the author.

21. Jenny Boyd and Holly George Warren, *Musicians in Tune: 75 Contemporary Musicians Discuss the Creative Process* (New York: Fireside, Simon and Schuster, 1992), 80.

Chapter Seven

1. The band first appeared in clubs on Long Island around 1967 as Soft White Underbelly. Four albums later, their most memorable song, "Don't Fear the Reaper," appeared on *The Agents of Fortune* (1976) and received wide airplay. Sandy Pearlman who, as a rock critic, is sometimes credited with having used the term "heavy metal," went on to manage the band.

2. See Martin Popoff, *Blue Oyster Cult: Secrets Revealed.* Listen to October 30, 2012, SONY Legacy, 17-CD boxed set. This coincided with Halloween, perhaps because of the Reaper. Currently, joining Bloom and Roeser are Jules Radino (drums), Richie Castellano (keyboard and guitar/background vocals) and Kasim Sultan (bass).

3. Bloom contributed "Black Blade" and "Veterans of the Psychic Wars" with Michael Moorcock. The science fiction author also wrote the lyrics for Hawkwind. This British psychedelic hard rock band dwelled in mythic stories. Their work included *In Search of Space* (1971), *Space Ritual* (1973), and *Warrior on the Edge* (1975).

4. An interview with Alexander Laurance in 1994 John Shirley observes that he and Bruce Sterling had done "Parallel Work." http:/www.blueoystercult.com.

5. Ursula K. Le Guin, *The Dispossessed: An Ambiguous Utopia* (New York: Harper and Row, 1974), 257.

6. Mircea Eliade, *Myth and Reality*, trans. Willard Trask (New York: Harper Torchbooks, 1968), 452.

7. Eliade, 453, 455.

8. Eliade, 455.

9. *Ibid.*

10. Eliade, 456.

11. Stanton Marian (Duquesne University diss. 1981, 227) is cited in *Shamanism: An Expanded View of Reality*, ed. Shirley Nicholson (Wheaton, IL: Quest, 1987), 269.

12. *Ibid.*

13. Eliade, 398.

14. Eliade, 401.

15. Eliade, 407.

16. Eliade, 456.

Chapter Eight

1. Nicole Biamonte offers a fascinating reading of "Cygnus X-1" from *A Farewell to Kings* she points out how the music patterns the storyline. "Contre

Nous," *Rush and Philosophy: Heart and Mind United*, ed. Jim Berti and Durrell Bowman (Chicago: Open Court/Carus, 2011), 196.

2. Deena Weinstein, *The Artistic Vision of Modern Society in Rush, Pink Floyd, and Bruce Springsteen* (Montreal: New World Perspectives, 1985).

3. Timothy Smolko, "What Can This Strange Device Be?" *Rush and Philosophy*, 228.

4. Chris McDonald, "Open Secrets, Individualism, and Middle Class Identity in the Songs of Rush," *Popular Music and Society* 31 (2008): 319.

5. Michio Kaku, *Physics of the Impossible* (New York: Doubleday, 2008), 31.

6. Dan Nooger, "Rush Goes into Future Shock: Music Will Not Exist in 2112," *Circus* (April 27, 1976).

7. Durrell Bowman, "More than They Bargained For," *Rush and Philosophy*, 170. He lists Lee's instruments on these albums as Minimoog, Oberheim OBX-a, and Roland Jupiter 8.

8. Durrell Bowman comments on Paul Theberge, *Any Sound You Can Imagine*, and H. Stith Bennett, "Notation and Identity in Contemporary Popular Music," *Popular Music* 3 (1983): 231. See *Rush and Philosophy*, 177.

9. Bowman, 188.

10. Bowman, 179.

11. Mark Poster, *The Mode of Information: Poststructuralism and the Social Context* (Chicago: University of Chicago Press and Cambridge: Polity, 1990), 4.

12. Poster, 7.

13. Poster, 9.

14. Rodney Brooks, "Making Living Systems," *Science at the Edge: Conversations with the Leading Scientific Thinkers Today*, ed. John Brockman (New York: Union Square, 2008), 51.

15. Poster, 15.

16. Neil Peart, *Ghost Rider* (Toronto: ECW, 2002), 258–262. Peart offers his recommendations for adapting to difficult circumstances.

Chapter Nine

1. Following the first album they were signed to Clive Davis's new record label, Arista Records. A series of successful albums followed: *I, Robot* (1977), *Pyramid* (1978), *Turn of a Friendly Card* (1980), *Eye in the Sky* (1982), *Ammonia Avenue* (1984), *Vulture Culture* (1985), *Stereotomy* (1986), and *Gaud* (1987).

2. *I, Robot* (1977) liner notes. The robot theme appears in Styx's *Kilroy Was Here* with "Mr. Roboto." The Flaming Lips created "Yoshimi Battles the Pink Robots."

3. Stephen Holden, *The Village Voice*, August 29, 1977, 38. The album also had a song called "The Voice." It has a robotized warning speaking over the sound of the bass.

4. Cited by Gary K. Wolfe, *The Known and the Unknown: The Iconography of Science Fiction* (Kent, OH: Kent State University Press, 1979), 158.

5. "Electric Eye" by Judas Priest has a similar theme and is examined by Robert Walser (164). The song, which appears on *Screaming for Vengeance* (1982), is described as conveying music codes of power and danger with a scrambling guitar solo and syncopated choruses that attempt to defy "solid metric organization." "The song ends with feedback and echo, like a science fiction movie soundtrack accompanying a view of space—vast, mysterious, and ineffable" (164).

6. Stephen Thomas Erlewine, review of *The Eye in the Sky*, All Music Reviews, www.allmusicreviews.com.

7. Stan McDaniel, "The Coalescence of Minds," *Philosophers Look at Science Fiction*, ed. Nicholas D. Smith (Chicago: Nelson Hall, 1982), 118–19.

8. Teilhard de Chardin, *The Future of Man* (New York: Pyramid, 1966), 116.

9. de Chardin, 120. For Teilhard, the scientist-priest, who refers to evolving consciousness as *Noogenesis*, this leads, in a religious sense, toward *Christogen-*

esis, which would be the redemption of the evolutionary past.

10. Olaf Stapledon, *Last and First Men*, 1933, 224. "The More Complex the Form the More Percipient and Active the Spirit," 34. Also see 231.

11. Arthur C. Clarke, cited. in *Philosophers Look at Science Fiction*, ed. Nicholas Smith (Chicago: Nelson Hall, 1982), 122.

Coda

1. See Jean Baudrillard, *Simulacra and Simulation* (1981), Frederic Jameson, *Postmodernism and the Logic of Late Capitalism* (1991), Brian McHale, *Postmodern Fiction* (1987) and *Constructing Postmodernism* (1992), Douglas Kellner and Steve Best, *The Postmodern Turn* (1997) and *The Postmodern Adventure* (2001). The emphasis placed upon simulation and simulacra in postmodern society by a theorist like Jean Baudrillard finds a complement in an artist like this, as well as in stories of virtual reality, computing and electronic identities, and digital global networks. Fragmentation and de-centering of the subject are aspects postmodernism, as is simulation. Bowie engaged in all of this. Frederic Jameson has presented postmodernism as a crisis in representation.

2. Gerald Alva Miller, Jr., *Exploring the Limits of the Human Through Science Fiction* (New York: Palgrave, 2012), 3.

3. Miller, 12–13.

4. Larry McCaffrey, 3.

5. Carlen Lavigne, *Cyberpunk Women: Feminism and Science Fiction: A Critical Study* (Jefferson, NC: McFarland, 2013).

6. Simon Frith, 1987 essay, 461–62; see *Music for Pleasure: Essays on the Sociology of Pop* (Cambridge: Polity and New York: Routledge, 1988). *Taking Popular Music Seriously* (2007) collects some of his essays. In his essays he makes use of symbolic interactionism and Marxist theory.

7. Frith, *Sound Effects*, 1983, 272.

8. Edward Macan, *Rocking the Classics* (New York: Oxford University Press, 1997), 145.

9. Greil Marcus, *Mystery Train*, 6th ed. (New York: Plume, 2015).

10. Miller, 18.

11. *Ibid.*

12. Miller, xii.

13. Miller, 1–2.

14. Carl Freeman, 32. Miller cites Carl Freeman's assertion that "science fiction is determined by the dialectic between estrangement and cognition," pp. 16–17. Steven Shaviro (ix), cited by Miller, 7. Gary K. Wolfe, *How Great Science Fiction Works*, 175–180, 184.

15. Miller, 7.

Bibliography

Abrahams, I. *Hawkwind: Sonic Assassins*. London: SAF, 2004.

Adorno, Theodor. "On the Fetish Character in Music and the Regression of Listening" (1938). In *Essays on Music*, ed. R. Leppert, trans. S.A. Gillespie. Berkeley: University of California Press, 2002.

_____. "The Schema of Mass Culture." In *The Culture Industry*. New York: Routledge, 1991.

Aldiss, Brian. *The Billion Year Spree: The True History of Science Fiction*. New York: Schocken, 1974.

Anderson, Kevin J., and Neil Peart. *Clockwork Angels*. Toronto: ECW, 2012.

Asimov, Isaac. *The Foundation Trilogy*. New York: Avon, 1974.

_____. *I, Robot*. New York: Random House, 1950. Reprint, New York: Bantam/Spectra, 2008.

Atheling, William, Jr. [James Blish]. *More Issues at Hand*. Chicago: Advent, 1970.

Atteburg, Brian, and Veronica Hollinger. *Parabolas of Science Fiction*. Middletown, VT: Wesleyan University Press, 2013.

Auden, W.H. *The Enchafed Flood, or Romantic Iconography of the Se*a. New York: Random House, 1950.

Auslander, Philip. *Performing Glam Rock: Gender and Theatricality in Popular Music*. Ann Arbor: University of Michigan Press, 2006.

Auxier, Randall E. "Magic Pages and Mythic Plants," *Led Zeppelin and Philosophy*, ed. Scott Calif. Chicago: Open Court, 2009.

Ballard, J.G. *Crash*. New York: Farrar, Straus, 1973.

Barron, Frank. *Creativity and Personal Freedom*. New York: D. Van Nostrand, 1968.

Barthes, Roland. *Mythologies*. London: Vintage, 2009.

Basche, Philip. *Heavy Metal Thunder*. San Francisco: Chronicle, 1985.

Bassy, Pascal. *Kraftwerk: Man, Machine, and Music*. London: SAF, 1993.

Beaver, Harold, ed. *The Science Fiction of Edgar Allan Poe*. Harmondsworth: Penguin, 1976.

Beer, John. *Coleridge the Visionary*. London: Chatto and Windus, 1959.

Benjamin, Walter. "The Work of Art in the Age of Mechanical Reproduction." In *Illuminations*. London: Fontana, 1973.

Berman, Michael. *Everyday Fantastic: Essays on Science Fiction and Human Being*. Cambridge: Cambridge University Press, 2008.

Bernal, J.D. *The World, the Flesh, and the Devil* (1929). London: Cape Editions, 1970.

Biamonte, Nicole. "Contre Nous." In *Rush and Philosophy: Heart and Mind United*, ed. Jim Berti and Durrell Bowman, 189–200. Chicago: Open Court/Carus, 2011.

Bibliography

Blish, James. *A Case of Conscience, in American Science Fiction: Five Classic Novels, 1956–1958*, ed. Gary K. Wolfe. New York: Library of America, 2012.

_____. *Cities in Flight*. New York: Avon, 1970. [*They Shall Have Stars, A Life for the Stars, Earthman Come Home, The Triumph of Time*.]

Bodkin, Maud. *Archetypal Patterns in Poetry*. Oxford: Clarendon, 1934.

Bourdieu, Pierre. *Distinction: A Social Critique of the Judgment of Taste*. London: Routledge, Kegan Paul, 1984.

Bowman, Durrell. "More Than They Bargained For." In *Rush and Philosophy*, ed. Jim Berti and Durrell Bowman, 169–188. Chicago: Open Court/Carus, 2011.

Boyd, Jenny, and Holly George Warren. *Musicians in Tune: Seventy-Five Contemporary Musicians Discuss the Creative Process*. New York: Fireside/Simon & Schuster, 1992.

Bracket, Leigh. Introduction. *The Best of Planet Stories*, vol. 1. New York: Random House, 1975.

Bradbury, Ray. *Fahrenheit 451*. New York: Simon & Schuster, 2013.

_____. *The Martian Chronicles*. New York: Simon & Schuster, 2012.

Brooks, Rodney "Making Living Systems." In *Science at the Edge: Conversations with the Leading Scientific Thinkers Today*, ed. John Brockman, 250–56. New York: Union Square/Sterling, 2008.

Brown, Mack. "A Star Comes Back to Earth." *Telegraph Magazine*, December 14, 1996, 304–316.

Bruford, Bill. *Yesyears: A Retrospective*. Videocassette. Vision Entertainment/Atlantic Record Corp., 1991.

Buckley, David. *Strange Fascination: David Bowie, The Definitive Story*. London: Virgin, 1999.

Burroughs, William S. *Soft Machine*. New York: Grove, 2011.

Cadigan, Pat. *Ultimate Cyberpunk*. New York: Ibooks, 2002.

Cagle, Van. *Reconstructing Pop/Subculture: Art, Rock, and Andy Warhol*. Thousand Oaks and London: Sage, 1995.

Calif, Scott, ed. *Led Zeppelin and Philosophy*. Chicago: Open Court, 2009.

Campbell, Joseph. *The Hero with a Thousand Faces*. Princeton: Princeton University Press, 1949.

Campbell, Joseph, and Bill Moyers. *The Power of Myth*. New York: Anchor, 1991.

Capek, Karel. *R.U.R. (Rossum's Universal Robots)*, trans. Claudia Novak-Jones. New York: Penguin Classics, 2004.

Caroti, Simone. *The Generation Starship: A Critical History 1934–2001*. Jefferson, NC: McFarland, 2011.

Chapman, Ian. "Ziggy's Urban Alienation: Assembling the Heroic Outsider." In *Enchanting David Bowie: Space, Time, Body, Memory*, ed. Toija Cinque, Christopher Moore, and Sean Redmond. London: Bloomsbury, 2015.

Cherryh, C.J. *Down Below Station*. New York: DAW, 2001.

Christe, Ian. *Sound of the Beast: The Complete Headbanging History of Heavy Metal*. New York: HarperCollins, 2003.

Christgau, Robert. "Dark Side of the Moon." In *Rock Albums of the 70s*. New York: Da Capo, 1990.

Clarke, Arthur C. *Childhood's End*. (1953). New York: Del Rey, 1987.

_____. *The City and the Stars*. (1958). London: Gollancz, 2001.

Clerk, C. *The Saga of Hawkwind*. London: Omnibus, 2004.

Coates, Norma. "Revolution Now? Rock and the Political Potential of Gender." In

Bibliography

Sexing the Groove: Popular Music and Gender, ed. S. Whiteley London: Routledge, 1997.

Coleridge, Samuel Taylor. "Kublai Kahn." In *Coleridge.* London: Folio, 2003.

_____. "The Rime of the Ancient Mariner." In *Coleridge.* London: Folio, 2003.

Collins, Jon. *Rush Chemistry.* London: Helter Skelter, 2010.

Coxkill, Gordon. "David Bowie." *New Musical Express,* November 15, 1969.

Crosby, David, and Carl Gottlieb. *Long Time Gone.* New York: Doubleday, 1988, reprint 2007.

Curtis, Jim. *Rock Eras: Interpretation of Music and Society, 1954–1984.* Madison: University of Wisconsin Press, 1984.

Davenport, Basil. *The Science Fiction Novel: Imagination and Social Criticism.* Chicago: Advent, 1969.

Delany, Samuel R. *City of a Thousand Suns.* New York: Ace, 1965.

_____. *Dahlgren.* (1975). New York: Vintage, 2001.

_____. *The Einstein Intersection.* Middletown: Wesleyan University Press, 1998.

_____. *The Fall of the Towers.* New York: Ace, 1971.

_____. *The Jewel Hinged Jaw.* New York: Berkeley Windhover, 1978.

Delville, Michael. "The Moorcock/Hawkwind Connection." *Foundation* 62 (Winter 1994–95): 64–69.

Dick, Philip K. *The Eye in the Sky.* New York: Mariner, 2012.

_____. *The Man in the High Castle.* New York: Mariner, 2012.

Doggett, Peter. *The Man Who Sold the World: David Bowie in the 1970s.* New York: HarperCollins, 2012.

Doyle, Peter. *Echo and Reverb: Fabricating Space in Popular Music, 1900–1960.* Middletown: Wesleyan University Press, 2005.

Egan, Sean, ed. *Bowie on Bowie: Interviews and Encounters with David Bowie.* Chicago: Chicago Review, 2015.

Eliade, Mircea. *Myth and Reality,* trans. Willard Trask. New York: Harper Torchbooks, 1968.

_____. *Occultism, Witchcraft, and Cultural Fashions.* Chicago: University of Chicago Press, 1976.

Emerson, Keith. *Pictures of an Exhibitionist.* London: John Blake, 20003.

Fast, Susan. *In the Houses of the Holy: Led Zeppelin and the Power of Rock Music.* New York: Oxford University Press, 2001.

Felix, Justin. "That Space Cadet Glow: Science Fiction Narratives in Roger Waters's KAOS and Amused to Death." *Extrapolation* 41, no. 4 (Winter 2000): 375.

Ferkiss, Victor. *Technological Man.* New York: Mentor/New American Library, 1969.

Finney, Jack. *Invasion of the Body Snatchers.* (1954). New York: Charles Scribner's Sons, 1998.

Fitch, Richard. "In This Age of Grand Illusion: Bowie, Nihilism and Meaning." In *David Bowie: Critical Perspectives,* ed. Eoin Devereaux, Aileen Dillane, and Martin J. Power, 19–34. London: Routledge, 2015.

Forrester, George, Martyn Hanson, and Frank Askew. *Emerson, Lake and Palmer: The Show That Never Ends.* London: Helter Skelter, 2001.

Frank, Pat. *Alas, Babylon* (1959). New York: Harper Perennial, 2005.

_____. *Forbidden Area.* Philadelphia: Lippincott, 1956.

Frith, Simon. "David Bowie." *Let It Rock,* June 1973.

_____. *Music for Pleasure.* Cambridge: Cambridge University Press, 1988.

_____. *Performing Rites.* Cambridge: Harvard University Press, 1996.

_____. *Sound Effects: Youth, Leisure, and the Politics of Rock.* London: Constable, 1983.

Bibliography

_____. "The Suburban Sensibility: British Rock and Pop." In *Visions of Suburbia*, ed. Roger Silverstone, 269–79. London: Routledge, 1996.

Frye, Northrup. *Anatomy of Criticism*. Princeton: Princeton University Press, 1957.

_____. "The Archetypes of Literature." *Kenyon Review* 13, no. 1 (1951).

Gaiman, Neil. Foreword. Samuel R. Delaney, *Einstein Intersection*. Middletown: Wesleyan University Press, 1998.

Gibson, William. *Neuromancer*. New York: Ace, 1984.

_____. "Rocket and Radio." *Rolling Stone* 554 (June 15, 1989): 84.

Greene, Andy. "Inside Rush's Sci-Fi Opera." *Rolling Stone* 1160/1161 (July 5, 2012): 22.

Haldane, J.B.S. *Daedelus, or Science and the Future*. London: Kegan Paul, 1923.

Hall, Stuart, and Paddy Wannel. *The Popular Arts*. London: Hutchison, 1964.

Hamilton, Edith. *Mythology*. Boston and New York: Little, Brown, 1942.

Harris, James F. *Philosophy at 33 1/3 rpm: Themes in Classic Rock Music*. Chicago and La Salle: Open Court, 1993.

Haven, Richard. *Patterns of Consciousness: An Essay on Coleridge*. Amherst: University of Massachusetts Press, 1969.

Heinlein, Robert A. *Methusalah's Children*. (*Astounding* July, August, September 1941). New York: Gnome, 1958.

_____. *Orphans of the Sky*. (1951). New York: Baen, 2001.

_____. "Science Fiction: Its Nature, Faults, and Virtues." (1959). In *The Science Fiction Novel: Imagination and Social Criticism*, ed. Basil Davenport. Chicago: Advent, 1969.

_____. *Starship Troopers*. (1959). New York: Ace, 1987.

_____. *Stranger in a Strange Land*. (1961). New York: Ace, 1991.

Herbert, Frank. *Dune*. New York: Ace, 1990.

Hicks, Michael. *Sixties Rock: Garage, Psychedelia and Other Satisfactions*. Urbana: University of Illinois Press, 1999.

Holmes, Richard. *Coleridge, Early Visions, 1772–1804*. New York: Pantheon, 1989.

Holon-Hudson, Kevin. *Progressive Rock Reconsidered*. New York: Routledge, 2002.

Homer. *The Odyssey*, trans. Robert Fagels. New York: Penguin, 1990.

Hudson, Kevin Holan. *Progressive Rock Reconsidered*. London: Routledge, 2002.

Hull, Robot A. "Sounds and Visions: Psychedelia." *Creem* (January 1981). Also in *The Sound and the Fury: A Rock's Back Pages Reader*, ed. Barney Hoskins. New York: Bloomsbury, 2003.

Hung, Eric. "Hearing Emerson, Lake and Palmer Anew: Progressive Rock as Music of Attraction." *Current Musicology* 79–80 (Spring/Fall 2005): 245–59.

Huxley, Aldous. *The Letters of Aldous Huxley*, ed. Grover Smith. Cambridge: Harvard University Press, 1969.

Huyssen, Andreas. *After the Great Divide: Modernism, Mass Culture, Postmodernism*. Basingstoke: Macmillan, 1986.

Ihde, Erin. "Do Not Panic: Hawkwind, the Cold War and 'the Imagination of Disaster.'" *Cogent Arts and Humanities* (March 2015): 1–13. http://www.cogentoa,tandfonline.com, accessed July 2, 2015.

Jensen, George. *Post-Jungian Criticism*. Albany: State University of New York Press, 2003.

Jones, James T. "Sharing a Shadow." *Post-Jungian Criticism: Theory and Practice*, ed. James S. Baumlin, Tita French Baumlin, and George H. Jensen. Albany: State University of New York Press, 2004.

Jones, Steve. *Pop Music and the Press*. Philadelphia: Temple University Press, 1974.

Bibliography

Jung, C.G. *Flying Saucers: A Modern Myth of Things Seen in the Skies*, trans. R.F.C. Hull. New York: Harcourt Brace, 1959.

_____. *Memories, Dreams, Reflections*, ed. Anelia Jaffe, trans. Richard and Clara Winston. New York: Random House, 1961. Reprint, New York: Vintage, 1989.

Kaku, Michio. *Physics of the Impossible: A Scientific Exploration in the World of Phasers, Force Fields, Teleportation, and Time Travel*. New York: Doubleday, 2008.

Kaye, Lenny. "Flying Saucers and Rock and Roll." *Locus* 5 (September 16, 1972): 6.

_____. "The Tattooed Dragon Meets the Wolfman." Exhibition of Mimeographed Fanzines. New York Book Fair, 2014. www.thoughtcatalog.com.

Kennedy, Victor. *Strange Brew: Metaphors of Magic and Science in Rock Music*. Newcastle-upon-Tyne: Cambridge Scholars, 2013.

Ketterer, David. *New Worlds for Old: The Apocalyptic Imagination. Science Fiction, and American Literature*. Garden City: Doubleday Anchor, 1974.

Knight, Damon. "To Serve Man." *Galaxy Science Fiction* (November 1961). In *Far Out*. New York: Simon & Schuster, 1961.

Knight, G. Wilson. *The Starlit Dome*. Oxford: Clarendon, 1941.

Kohl, Paul R. Review of Edward Macan, *Endlesss Enigma: A Musical Biography of Emerson Lake and Palmer*. *Popular Music and Society* 32, no. 3 (July 2009): 437–39.

Kramer, Lawrence. *Musical Meaning: Toward a Critical History*. Berkley: University of California Press, 2001.

Kuhn, Thomas S. *The Structure of Scientific Revolutions*. Chicago: University of Chicago Press, 1970.

Laing, Dave. *The Sound of Our Time*. London: Sheed and Ward, 1969.

_____. "The World's Best Rock Read: Let It Rock 1972–75." *Popular Music and Society* 33, no. 4 (2010): 449–63.

Laing, Dave, Marshall Lee, and Derek B. Scott. *Popular Music Matters*. Burlington, VT: Ashgate, 2014.

Larson, R.D. *Musique Fantastique*. Metuchen, NJ: Scarecrow, 1985.

Lavigne, Carlen. *Cyberpunk Women, Feminism and Science Fiction: A Critical Study*. Jefferson, NC: McFarland, 2013.

LeGuin, Ursula. Introduction. *The Norton Book of Science Fiction*, ed. Ursula Le Guin and Brian Attebery. New York: W.W. Norton, 1997.

_____. *The Left Hand of Darkness*. New York: Ace, 2000.

Lehan, Richard. *The City in Literature*. Berkeley: University of California Press, 1998.

Leigh, Wendy. *Bowie: The Biography*. New York and London: Gallery, 2014.

Letts, Marianne Tatom. *Radiohead and the Resistant Concept Album*. Bloomington: Indiana University Press, 2012.

Lewis, C.S. "On Science Fiction." In *Of Other Worlds: Essays and Stories*, ed. Walter Hooper and Geoffrey Bles. London: Bles, 1966.

Lowes, John Livingston. *The Road to Xanadu: A Study in the Ways of the Imagination*. Boston: Houghton Mifflin, 1927.

Lupro, Michael Mooradian. "Keeping Space Fantastic: The Transformative Journey of Major Tom." In *Enchanting David Bowie: Space, Time, Body, Memory*, ed. Toija Cinque, Christopher Moore, and Sean Redmond. London: Bloomsbury, 2015.

Macan, Edward. *Endless Enigma: A Musical Biography of Emerson, Lake, and Palmer*. Chicago: Open Court, 2006.

_____. *Rocking the Classics*. Oxford and New York: Oxford University Press, 1997.

MacDonald, Bruno, ed. *Pink Floyd: Through the Eyes of the Band, Its Fans and Foes*. New York: Da Capo, 1997.

Bibliography

MacLeod, Donald. "Axeman/Astrophysicist Brian May Named University Chancellor." *The Guardian,* November 17, 2007.

Maltby, Richard. Introduction. *Dreams for Sale: Popular Culture in the Twentieth Century,* ed. Richard Maltby. London: Harrup, 1989.

Marcus, Greil. *Mystery Train,* 6th ed. New York: Plume, 2015.

Martin, Bernice. "The Sacralization of Disorder: Symbolism in Rock Music." *Sociology of Religion* (1979).

Martin, Bill. *Listening to the Future: The Time of Progressive Rock.* Chicago: Open Court, 1998.

_____. *Music of Yes: Structure and Vision in Progressive Rock.* Chicago: Open Court, 1996.

Maslow, Abraham. *Religions, Values, and Peak Experiences.* New York: Viking Penguin, 1970. Reprint, 1987.

May, Rollo. *The Courage to Create.* New York: W.W. Norton, 1975. Reprint, New York: Bantam, 1985.

McCaffrey, Larry. *Storming the Reality Studio.* Durham, NC: Duke University Press, 1991.

McDaniel, Stan. "The Coalescence of Minds." In *Philosophers Look at Science Fiction,* ed. Nicholas D. Smith. Chicago: Nelson Hall, 1982.

McDonald, Chris. "Open Secrets, Individualism, and Middle-Class Identity in the Songs of Rush." *Popular Music and Society* 31 (2008): 319.

McGann, Jerome. *The Romantic Ideology.* Chicago: University of Chicago Press, 1984

McGraw-Hill Concise Encyclopedia of Science and Technology, 5th ed. New York: McGraw-Hill, 2005.

McKinney, Angus. "The Future Isn't What It Used to Be." *New Musical Express,* September 13, 1986: 102–139.

McLeod, Ken. Review of Edward Macan, *Endless Enigma: A Musical Biography of Emerson, Lake, and Palmer. Notes* (June 207): 874–76.

_____. "Space Oddities: Aliens, Futurism, and Meaning in Popular Music," *Popular Music* 22, no. 3, 337–55.

McRobbie, Angela. "Notes on What Happened to W- and Post-Feminist Symbolic Violence." In *The Aftermath of Feminism: Gender, Culture, and Social Change,* 124–49. London: Sage, 2009.

Meisel, Perry. *The Cowboy and the Dandy: Crossing Over from Romanticism to Rock and Roll.* New York and Oxford: Oxford University Press, 1998.

Meyer, Leonard. *Emotion and Meaning in Music.* Chicago: University of Chicago Press, 1956.

Middleton, Richard. Review, *Piper at the Gates of Dawn* (44–45). *Pop Music and the Blues* (Fall 1967).

Miles. Review of *A Saucerful of Secrets. International Times* (August 8, 1968).

Moorcock, Michael. *The Black Corridor.* Frogmore: Granada, 1969.

Morris, Chris. "Lynne Zooms Back to ELO with Epic Disc." *Billboard* 163, no. 4 (June 15, 2001).

Moskowitz, Sam. "How Science Fiction Got Its Name." *The Magazine of Fantasy and Science Fiction* (1957). In *Explorers of the Infinite: Shapers of Science Fiction,* ed. Sam Moskowitz. New York: Meridian, 1959.

Mullen, Richard D. "The Earthmanist Culture: Cities in Flight as a Spenglerian History." Afterword to *Cities in Flight* by James Blish. New York: Avon, 1970.

Mumford, Lewis. *The Pentagon of Power: The Myth of the Machine.* New York: Harcourt Brace Jovanovich, 1970.

Bibliography

Murray, Charles Shaar. "Goodbye Ziggy and a Big Hello to Aladdin Sane." *New Musical Express,* January 27, 1973. In *Bowie on Bowie: Interviews and Encounters with David Bowie,* ed. Sean Egan, 25–35. Chicago: Chicago Review, 2015.

Myers, Paul. *A Wizard, a True Star: Todd Rundgren in the Studio.* London: Jawbone, 2010.

Nash, Graham. *Wild Tales: A Rock and Roll Life.* New York: Crown, 2013.

Nooger, Dan. "Rush Goes Into Future Shock: Music Will Not Exist in 2112." *Circus* (April 27, 1976).

Olderman, Raymond. *Beyond the Waste Land: A Study in the American Novel of the Nineteen Sixties.* New Haven: Yale University Press, 1972.

Orwell, George. *1984.* New York: Harcourt, Brace, 1983.

Peart, Neil. *Ghost Rider: Travels on the Healing Road.* Toronto: ECW, 2002.

Pegg, Nicholas. *The Complete David Bowie.* London: Reynolds and Acorn, 2002. Reprint, London: Titan, 2011.

Polyani, Michael, and Harry Prosch. *Meaning.* Chicago: University of Chicago Press, 1975.

Poster, Mark. *The Mode of Information: Poststructuralism and Social Context.* Chicago: University of Chicago Press and Cambridge: Polity, 1990.

Power, Martin J., Eoin Devereux, Aileen Dillane. "Where Are We Now? Contemporary Scholarship on David Bowie." In *David Bowie: Critical Perspectives.* London and New York: Routledge, 2015.

Prince, Michael J. "The Science Fiction Protocols of Frank Zappa: Problems of Genre and Satire in Billy the M_____, Joe's Garage, and Thing Fish." *Chapter and Verse* (Spring 2005) www.popmatters.com.

Reich, Charles A. *The Greening of America.* New York: Random House, 1970.

Reid, Nancy "Clinging to the Edge of Magic: The Shamanic Aspects of The Grateful Dead." *Perspectives on The Grateful Dead,* ed. Robert G. Weiner and Rebecca G. Adams. Westport, CT: Greenwood, 1999.

Rose, Phil. Interview with Roger Waters (February 28, 1995) in *Roger Waters and Pink Floyd: The Concept Albums.* Madison, NJ: Fairleigh Dickinson University Press, 2015.

Roszak, Theodore. *Making of the Counter Culture* (1969). Berkeley: University of California Press, 1995.

_____. *Where the Wasteland Ends.* New York: Bantam, Doubleday, Dell, 1970

Russ, Joanna. *The Female Man.* (1975). Boston: Beacon, 2000.

_____. "Speculations: The Subjunctivity of Science Fiction." *Extrapolations* 15, no. 1 (December 1973): 52.

_____. "Towards an Aesthetic of Science Fiction." *Science Fiction Studies* 2, Part 2 (July 1975): 112–18.

Sanjek, David. The Bloody Heart of Rock and Roll: Images of Popular Music in Contemporary Speculative Fiction." *Journal of Popular Culture* 28, no. 4 (Spring 1995): 179–209.

Schindler, Scott. "Pink Floyd." In *Icons of Rock: An Encyclopedia of the Legends Who Changed Music Forever,* vol. 2, ed. Scott Schindler and Andy Schwartz. Westport, CT, and London: Greenwood, 2008.

Schippers. Mimi. *Rockin' Out of the Box: Gender Maneuvering in Alternative Hard Rock.* New Brunswick, NJ: Rutgers University Press, 2002.

Scholes, Robert. *Structural Fabulation: An Essay on Fiction of the Future.* South Bend: University of Notre Dame Press, 1975.

Bibliography

Seay, Davin, and Mary Neely. *Stairway to Heaven: The Spiritual Roots of Rock n' Roll*. New York: Ballantine, 1986.

Shaffner, Nicholas. *Saucerful of Secrets: The Pink Floyd Odyssey*. New York: Dell, 1991.

Shelley, Mary. *Frankenstein*. New York and Oxford: Oxford University Press, 2009.

Shipston, Roy. "Are Spacemen Floyd on Their Way Back to Earth?" *Disc and Music Echo*, November 22, 1969.

Shirley, John. "Science Fiction and Rock Music." *Metaphores* 9–10 (April 1984).

Silverberg, Robert. *The Science Fiction Hall of Fame, vol. 1, 1929–1964*. New York: Orb, 2005.

Sinclair, David. "Station to Station." *Rolling Stone*, June 10, 1993. In *Bowie on Bowie: Interviews and Encounters with David Bowie*, ed. Sean Egan, 231–48. Chicago: Chicago Review, 2015.

Skeggs, Beverly. *Formation of Class and Gender: Becoming Respectable*. London: Sage, 1977.

Slavca, Neil. *Electric Don Quixote: The Definitive Story of Frank Zappa*. London: Omnibus, 2003.

Smith, Nicholas D. *Philosophers Look at Science Fiction*. London: Burnham, 1982.

Smolko, Timothy. "What Can This Strange Device Be?" In *Rush and Philosophy: Heart and Mind United*, ed. Jim Berti and Durrell Bowman, 225–238. Chicago: Open Court/Carus, 2011.

Snow, C.P. *The Two Cultures and the Scientific Revolution*. Rede Lecture, 1959.

Spitz, Marc. *Bowie: A Biography*. New York: Crown/Archetype, 2010.

Stableford, Bill. *Science Fact, Science Fiction*. London: Routledge, 2006.

Stambler, Irwin. *Pop, Rock, Soul*. New York: St. Martin's, 1974.

Stamp. Paul. *The Music's All That Matters: A History of Progressive Rock*. London: Quartet, 1997.

Stapledon, Olaf. *Last and First Men*. (1930). Mineola, NY: Dover, 2008.

Stenning, Paul. *Iron Maiden: Thirty Years of the Beast*. Chicago: Independent Publishers, 2006.

Stevenson, Nick. *David Bowie: Fame, Sound and Vision*. Cambridge: Polity, 2006.

Sterling, Bruce. *Tomorrow Now: Envisioning the Next Fifty Years*. New York: Random House, 2003.

_____. *Zeitgeist*. New York: Spectra, 2001.

_____, ed. *Mirrorshades: An Anthology of Cyberpunk*. London and New York: Palladin Books, 1986.

Storey, John. *Cultural Theory and Popular Culture: A Reader*. London: Pearson, 2006.

Stump, Paul. *The Music's All That Matters: A History of Progressive Rock*. London: Quartet Books, 1997.

Sturgeon, Theodore. *The Complete Stories of Theodore Sturgeon*. Berkeley: North Atlantic, 1997.

Tamarkin, Jeff. *The Turbulent Flight of Jefferson Airplane*. New York: Simon & Schuster, 2003.

Tauber, Alfred I. *Science and the Quest for Meaning*. Waco, TX: Baylor University Press, 2009.

Toffler, Alvin. *Future Shock*. New York: Vintage, 1970.

Tribbe, Matthew D. *No Requiem for the Space Age: The Apollo Moon Landings and American Culture*. New York: Oxford University Press, 2014.

Trynka, Paul. *David Bowie: Starman*. New York and Boston: Little, Brown, 2011.

Bibliography

Van Elferen, I. *Gothic Music: Sounds of the Uncanny.* Cardiff: University of Wales Press, 2012.

Wakeman, Rick, and Martin Roach. *Grumpy Old Rock Star and Other Wondrous Stories.* London: Preface, 2008.

Waldrop, Sheldon. *The Aesthetics of Self-Invention: Oscar Wilde to David Bowie.* Minneapolis: University of Minnesota Press, 2004.

Wall, Mick. *Run to the Hills.* London: Sanctuary, 2004.

Walser, Robert. *Running With the Devil: Power, Gender, and Madness in Heavy Metal Music.* Middleton, CT: Wesleyan University Press, 1993.

Watts, Michael. "Oh, You Pretty Things." *Melody Maker* 22 (January 1972).

Weinstein, Deena. *Heavy Metal: The Music and Its Culture.* New York: Da Capo, 1991. Reprint, 2000.

_____. *Serious Rock: The Artistic Vision of Modern Society in Rush, Pink Floyd and Bruce Springsteen.* Montreal: New World Perspectives, 1985.

Wells, H.G. *The Time Machine.* New York: Penguin Classics, 2005.

_____. *The War of the Worlds. A Critical Edition of the War of the Worlds: H.G. Wells's Scientific Romance,* ed. Harry M. Geduld and David Y. Hughes. Bloomington: Indiana University Press, 1993.

Westfahl, Gary. *The Mechanics of Wonder: The Creation of Science Fiction.* Liverpool: Liverpool University Press, 1998.

Whiteley, Sheila. *The Space Between the Notes: Rock and the Counterculture.* London and New York: Routledge, 2000.

Williams, Raymond. "The Analysis of Culture." In *Cultural Theory and Popular Culture: A Reader,* ed. John Storey. London: Pearson, 2006.

_____. "Base and Superstructure in Marxist Cultural Theory." In *Problems in Materialism and Culture.* London: Verso, 1980.

_____. *The Country and the City.* London: Chatto and Windus, 1973.

_____. *Culture and Society.* Harmondsworth: Penguin, 1963.

_____. "The Metropolis and the Emergence of Modernism." In *Unreal City: Urban Experiences in Modern European Literature and Art,* ed. David Kelley and Edward Timms. Manchester: Manchester University Press, 1985.

Willis, Ellen. *Beginning to See the Light: Sex, Hope, and Rock and Roll.* Jackson: University of Mississippi Press, 2012.

_____. *Out of the Vinyl Deeps: Ellen Willis on Rock Music.* Minneapolis: University of Minnesota Press, 2011.

Wolfe. Gary K. *American Science Fiction: Nine Classic Novels of the 1950s.* New York: Library of America, 2012.

_____. *How Great Science Fiction Works.* Chantilly, VA: The Great Courses, 2016.

_____. *The Known and the Unknown: The Iconography of Science Fiction.* Kent, OH: Kent State University Press, 1979.

Wragg, David. "Or Any Art At All: Frank Zappa Meets Critical Theory." *Popular Music* 2, no. 2 (2001): 205–222.

Zamyatin, Yvgeny. "Herbert Wells." In *H.G. Wells, The Critical Heritage,* ed. Patrick Parrinder, 260. London: Routledge, Kegan and Paul, 1972.

_____. *We.* (1924), trans. Natasha Randall. New York: Modern Library, 2006.

Zappa, Frank, and Peter Occhiogrosso. *The Real Frank Zappa Book.* New York: Simon & Schuster, 1989.

Zelazny, Roger. *Damnation Alley.* London: Sphere, 1971.

Zimmerman, Nadia. *Counterculture Kaleidoscope: Late 1960s San Francisco.* Ann Arbor: University of Michigan Press, 2009.

Index

Index

Index

Index

Index

Index